Shopping in the
Santa Monica Mall

Shopping in the Santa Monica Mall

The Journals of a Strolling Player

Steven Berkoff

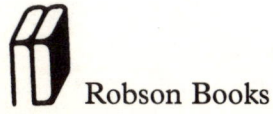
Robson Books

First published in Great Britain in 2000 by Robson Books,
10 Blenheim Court, Brewery Road, London N7 9NT

A member of the Chrysalis Group plc

Copyright © 2000 Steven Berkoff

The right of Steven Berkoff to be identified as author of this work has been asserted by him in accordance with the Copyright, Designs and Patents Act 1988

British Library Cataloguing in Publication Data

A catalogue record for this title is available from the British Library

ISBN 1 86105 357 6

All rights reserved. No part of this publication may be reproduced, stored in a retrieval system, or transmitted in any form or by any means, electronic, mechanical, photocopying, recording or otherwise, without the prior permission in writing of the publishers.

Typeset by FiSH Books, London
Printed by Butler & Tanner Ltd, Frome and London

For Clara

Contents

Introduction		ix
1	First Class?	1
2	'Godot' in Venice	6
3	Shopping in the Santa Monica Mall	11
4	*Salome* in Canterbury	17
5	*Salome* in Chicago	29
6	*Salome* in New York – The Last Performance	33
7	Rascals Deli – Miami	39
8	One-night Stand – Darlington	44
9	Samba in São Paulo	53
10	The Pool of Light	56
11	Bahamas	60
12	A Place Called Homestead	69
13	A Miami Health Club	83
14	The Explosion!	88
15	LA Story	101
16	A Face in the Crowd	112
17	Another Deli – Wolfies in Miami	122

18	Palm Springs	128
19	My Film: *Decadence*	134
20	Homage to the Hotel du Cap – Côte d'Azure	138
21	Breakfast at Itala's – Islington	143
22	Ha! Ha!	147
23	Christmas in the Caribbean	154
24	Bondi	161
25	Leaving Oz: In Memory of Brian Hagland	164
26	'Piss in the Sink Productions'	175
27	Letter from Israel	181
28	The Last Days of a Train Robber	185
29	The Killing Fields: Vilnius	190
30	Stanley Kubrick	198
31	Reid's Hotel – Madeira	207
32	Rio 2000	219

Introduction

Who can travel as much as an actor except a travelling salesman. A touring actor has to travel to survive reconstructing the whole play week after week, going from city to city, country to country. Theatres, streets and cities mark themselves indelibly in your mind, or as Tennessee Williams puts it so admirably, 'Cities swirled around me like dead leaves' – as Tom leaves home in Williams' moving play, *The Glass Menagerie*. That line as with so many of this playwright's lines strikes chords few other writers tend to reach. Film also whisks you to strange destinations and for longer periods, but unlike theatre where you are in control of your material to a great extent, in film you are a cog in a huge machine being inexorably wound round or ground down. The actor's or travelling player's life is akin to an explorer should the person be so inclined. The work then can take second billing to the opportunity of investigating the extraordinary planet on which we live. After a while one gets a feeling of a place and preferences: the cities one looks forward to revisiting and the other places that one shudders at returning to – and there are quite a few of those – however, even these offer up to the anthropologist's eye much fertile writing material. What I found to be strange, exotic or obscene in my travels is of course measured against the template of what I consider the norm. Since London has been my home for better or worse it has to be the standard from which other excesses are measured, particularly in America – the land of excess.

So what I see in the shopping mall in Santa Monica, though quite normal to the natives, has to be viewed according to my own point of view. On the other hand, exposure to some environments might make the UK seem like a prison of convention and miserable meanness, and the simple hedonistic environment of an LA diner becomes a kind of demi-paradise. The USA is of course an unending source of amusement and fascination since it has long abandoned what in the UK is regarded as the unwritten rules of civilised living. This in the UK does imply a certain restraint. In the USA there appears to be a touching belief in the infinite world of possibilities without limits. By contrast playing Oscar Wilde's *Salome*, which deals with extravagant excess and sexual promise, the local hotel in Canterbury was a mealy-mouthed dungeon of miserable meanness, where a plea to please turn off the epileptic fruit machine flashing away flagrantly was met with utter stupefaction and indifference.

Again the appalling life of the homeless vagrants on Venice Beach, Los Angeles is viewed with an eye used to the affirming nature of our welfare state, social security and public libraries in every borough (now sadly diminishing), a pub as opposed to a dark menacing cavern of a bar, although these too can be fascinating. Whilst in the States you are at first incredibly relieved to be out of the confining environment of Britain, 'thank god' you say to yourself as you enjoy a margarita in a simple cafe which would be impossible in your dreary pub whose staff can barely pull a pint and where you are turfed out unceremoniously at eleven. How pleasant to fill your car and not spend a fortune... how easy life can be... at times. How your vices are not taxed to death as if there is in Britain some unconscious or innate desire to penalise pleasure.

Introduction

Sometimes I write for the sheer joy of it or to give thanks to an experience that has so touched me that I feel impelled to record it, to set it down forever since these events will never be the same again. Like a conjugation of stars in a unique arrangement. Certain places have to be recorded like Wolfies Deli in Miami where several cultures can be seen jammed together: Jewish, American and East European, in metaphorically speaking one exotic sandwich.

A mini-series took me to Lithuania, a country which saw one of the very first blood baths of European Jewry on a scale unseen for centuries. These hideous programs started even before the Nazis had occupied the country and Lithuania became one of the first experiments in mass-killing for which the Nazis were duly famous. I visited what were the killing fields and it wasn't hard to imagine what abominations had taken place in that serene peaceful environment. Of course I had to set down my thoughts on that. So in a sense here is my bird's eye view of the world as I see it, feel it and even taste it.

My journey ends with New Year 2000 in Rio, where for once I was not to be whisked by film or touring theatre, but went for the simple pleasure of being in a city that was a home for me of sorts many years ago. This is where I met Ronnie Biggs on one of 'those' films in 1987. I revisited him after the old tearaway had suffered a stroke, which may have reminded him of his mortality. Whatever one may think of Ronnie Biggs, his legend in the minds of many is secure.

All those journeys, all those planes taking me safely to so many destinations. I'm truly grateful and wish to give a word of deep gratitude to the pilots who never come out of their cabin to take a curtain call. Well, Sir, you have my applause!

STEVEN BERKOFF

1
First Class?

I arrived in Los Angeles after American Airlines delivered me. A worse *First Class* I have never experienced and Economy might in some ways have actually been better (except when it's cattle-truck full of course, but in this case it wasn't). First Class is a tiny area in the front of the plane with a couple of dozen spongy seats covered with what looks like recycled dog fur of the kind you find in cheap minicabs that trawl for work in London's East End. The stewardesses, though well-meaning, looked like they would have been turned down at first base for a job in a Coney Island fast-food diner. They flopped around being pleasant but really wearing a mask of exhaustion and, while appreciating some of the merits of political correctness, I admit to the male chauvinist prejudice of liking a younger person to do a job where you must be nimble on your feet for a great deal of the time, especially on a flight from London to LA. Also, at that age oestrogen production diminishes at the same rate as patience, and a request to smoke my one cigarette of the flight in the smoking section, in which there was one seat available, is met with a curt, 'No, that's for the staff!' One saves energy at the autumn of one's life and why use ten words when five will do? I mean, am I travelling First Class or what? I couldn't accept the rude brevity of her response and sat there anyway and had a smoke for the five or six minutes it took me. However, the First Class area is so small, sealed off as it is by a thick curtain (always a source of wonderment to me as I spied it from Economy and imagined it populated by Arab sheikhs and movie stars, when in fact most of them look like Economy who have been upgraded by collecting their Air Miles) and being so enclosed it starts to remind me of Sartre's *Huis Clos* where Hell is other people. This small room was a perfect scenario for Hell in the air.

In Economy the sound of people's voices would at least be able to travel along the fuselage of the plane and get dissipated with a myriad other voices. However, in our First Class, squashy seats with the leg rests that keep rising and dropping, we could hear everything, every intimate detail of my neighbours' bronchial tract from the row behind and the row in front... the rasping, grinding syncopations from the nasal orifice as it trumpets the inner repulsive sounds of its phlegm-choked machinery.

To escape the rhythm that begins to drive you mad, you watch a movie and you do have a choice of your own video which is very cool and I watched Jim Carrey in *The Mask*. It's a tale that's brilliantly told about a man who finds his inner being when he is able to hide his face behind a mask and I immediately identify with this man who becomes wild, mischievous, demonic, surreal and a brilliant dancer to boot. The mask is the very thing we used to play with in our early drama classes since it would free us from the constraints that help us to 'adjust' to the norms of society. I can see why the film was so popular. But when *The Mask* was over, I still heard the croaking, flapping, coated chords fore and aft since in our curtained cocoon no sounds from those cheaper seats could penetrate and help to filter the audiophonic nightmare. Also the First Class snore is abundantly more thickly veneered from years of indulgence, cigars and booze which seem to add timbre and since one *was* allowed to smoke in the back row it turned the whole of First Class into a smoking section as thick wafts of the stuff flowed over all of us. They did not stop, and the smoke couldn't escape into Economy or Club and pollute them, no, the draped partition made us victims of each other, and so we shared their exhaled smoke between death rattles.

If the regularity of the snoring could be somehow tolerated by lowering your threshold of expectation and you managed to snatch forty winks, you would be abruptly torn out of that gentle oneiric web that was just forming to allow you to rest your head there when a loud vocalised yawn would tear it to shreds as the monster surfaced and felt some anally repressed desire to amplify his inner state and so we hear 'YAAAAAAAAAAAAGGHH.' He crows like he was in some filthy pig pen or at home farting on his sofa with a can of beer in his hand watching *Cheers*. Having then surfaced, he talks so loudly we how have to hear the boring workings of his brain after hearing for an hors-d'oeuvre the repulsive workings of his lungs and guts! I was beginning to feel like the killer in the Poe story *The Tell-Tale Heart* who felt compelled to murder a poor man whose only offence was to possess an unfortunately loathsome eye that filled the killer with dread. Plane rage!

So, not being able to sleep, I wrote a short story about an unemployed actor which was so thoroughly sad and depressing that I thought it rather good since I was in that kind of mood. By then some utterly tasteless chicken was being served with a sauce as a late-night nosh before landing. North America stretched out before us, covered by a huge eiderdown of cloud. It almost seemed like a gigantic lake that licked against the peaks that just broke through them. I never could understand how a canopy of cloud could be so flat. Now as I examine the rest of the occupants I notice two women, who look like sisters, periodically put their napkins over their faces in some kind of ritualistic act, I thought, since they now looked like women from a harem. Perhaps this eccentricity is peculiar to sisters of a rather more than plain demeanour and for whom the world of 'family' is something they have acclimatised themselves never to desire. In fact they looked like a pair of friendly hens. I solved the puzzle when I realised they were making a kind of visual protest against the smokers behind them. When not doing this harem action, one was engaged in doing needlework on a cloth that you buy with a design printed on it and therefore creativity is fulfilled by sewing in the colours. This particular one had a large cat's face printed on it. During the entire journey they both continually snacked or ate the love that had been denied them.

Fortunately the traveller who sat next to me on the window seat was an elegant, middle-aged gentleman who slept most of the time but on waking shared some conversation about satellite dishes and the day arriving when we will be able to tune into five hundred channels. When I was pushed to reveal my own ways of earning a living he admitted that he already knew me from 'movies'. I did admit to an anachronistic compulsion to act on stage as if this were a quaint old cottage industry that one performed more for the pleasure of supporting ancient trades. I felt like some white-haired old craftsman, painfully but faithfully turning out hand-tooled brass fittings.

On planes particularly, the response, when asked what I do, is always deep respect for the live theatre, usually manifested by an admission of having seen *Cats*! 'Couldn't get tickets for the *Phantom* on Saturday night [his obviously preferred night of theatre going] for six months.' Live theatre in their minds is, after all, the equivalent of a night of Andrew Lloyd Webber. Drama for them is a movie. Theatre is now the big effects musical in the same way that circus is elephants, tigers and clowns. Still it is, in the end, merely a way of making conversation with someone who sat next to you for ten hours of your life and who you will never see again. I, in turn, learned about the density of snow in the Northern California regions and how good it was for hiking. He was a pure American, slim, fit, silver-haired and an expert in his field of satellite communications... I was relieved when we landed with ne'er a tremble.

2
'Godot' in Venice

Venice Bums

A little early morning jog turns everything on. After the run I stop for a coffee at what I have baptised the *Waiting for Godot* Café and am served by Mimi, a wide-faced, beautiful and sensual Eurasian who works there. All the crazies were in, just hanging out and fiddling with nothing. It's the last café on the beach before Venice turns gratefully into Santa Monica. It faces a large car park where some of them sleep and the more fortunate have old vans that are their homes and have been for years. When they wake they stretch, scratch and wobble to this café and hang out. An oldish woman is presenting the habits of normality by digging in a red plastic vanity bag. It's torn and dusty and she shakes out the last vestiges that attach her to civilisation, an old toothbrush, a comb and some other unnamable detritus that she may have found in a garbage bin. A black man with broken teeth directs her activities as if he had some authority over her thus giving him some status over the bottom rung.

These people are always yelling and cursing as if everything is of the utmost consequence or else it's just a way of burning off that exuberant morning energy before lethargy sets in. Others stand outside the store, a still-life painting, as if they had been set down there from another planet and have been disconnected from the mother ship. They stand gripping their polystyrene cups and blinking in the early morning sunlight with nothing to do and nowhere to go but live 'Godot'-like existences, which means from second to second. They have fallen through the safety net of society, through the grill, and have nothing material to offer the world not even a healthy working body and so, like sediment, they gather on the bottom, stirring themselves out of their dirty, worn duvets and picking at the junk they have acquired in their shopping trolleys. Their carts are usually full, piled to the top with the scoopings-out of the bins that line the alleyways along the boardwalk. These giant metal containers are always crammed full of surplus waste, undesired food, left-over pizzas, crusts, giros, tacos, burritos, dogs, bagels and paper plates with bits of cheese stuck on and ready to be scraped off with hungry, blackened nails. I hear them at night from my hotel room as they crawl into the large bins like giant slugs, for many of these homeless have grown fat on scraps of compulsive eating.

I returned one night clutching my cup of 'to go' cappuccino as I couldn't bear to see the rip-roaring sunset from my balcony without a coffee in my hand. I could then watch God's furnaces being closed down for the night whilst sipping delicately. On this particular night in the darkening shadows of the ammonia-stinking alleyway I saw a human being impersonating a slimy maggot and foraging in the rotting garbage, but it was the isolation of the man that was the worst of it. If there had been a few working together at least there would be a solidarity in their insufferable squalor but he looked terribly alone as he heaved himself over the edge of the filthy bin and plunged his hands into God knows what human effluvium. His fat belly hung over his grimy jeans and his face was red and blotchy with sores.

Meanwhile round the corner in Gold's Gym the shiny bodies work at being beautiful and fret over their extra ounces. In the gym's store they pick through multi-coloured leotards and cut-off T-shirts with prints of perfect human specimens emblazoned on the front, bodies rippling with health and impossibly sculptured façades. But outside the 'Godot's' Café they wait, sit, stand and exchange bits of basic banter and useful info on where to get the crusts of life, the gritty reality of basic needs like a cigarette and a coffee. Whereas higher up the road, since you already have the basics, you therefore choose refinements of these needs. At ground level you try to get up with the sun to give the impression that there is something to get up for, whilst the others, the hopeless and the despairing, stay huddled within their dirty blankets and will not rise for the sun but only when dire necessity calls them to eat, drink or relieve themselves. For many it is a joy to leave their hard, unforgiving, concrete beds and rise with those of Beverly Hills since it is the same sun that blesses both, as Coriolanus might say. So you get up with the world, go to the corner deli and 'meet and greet'.

Many here have fallen even below the level of the crust. Corrosion has rusted the wires in their heads and these creatures can be seen wandering around aimlessly or engaging in small obsessive rituals. One young man is picking up bits of paper and scraps as if he were the boardwalk cleaner and then wiping round the base of the dustbins, clearing away the dirt and mud. He does it fussily, on his knees, like it might be his proudly kept, little front lawn. He needs to keep on doing it in order to dull some creative act of will. There are many brain-damaged souls like him as the undercrust come out here to rest and rot and be ignored by the state. They go through a variety of moods: excited, crazed, feeble, eccentric, obsessive and silent and act in a way normally never seen outside institutions. It is as if someone had opened the gates of bedlam and they have all come pouring out, in all the varieties that exist of human aberrations, and have found little holes and crannies in Venice.

Another young black man walks up and down, a slow pointless walk, wearing a skirt and carrying a little plastic bag over his arm, then he sits and slowly scratches his head. Another dresses as if for an Arctic expedition with a great army coat, hood, dark glasses and yet wearing his earphones. He continuously stands rock-still and as I pass the creature I hear a young girl's voice ring out, 'A little change, please, mister?' I turn and the man's hand is out and cupped for the hoped-for coins but he is staring straight ahead disclaiming, so to speak, any responsibility for the weird voice. 'Why do you speak like that?' I asked, since my familiarity with so many homeless makes me more at ease with this low society. I approached the strange being as these 'ragged ghosts' fascinate me and I am curious to know what brought them to this. I gave him some change and he said, 'Thank you,' in a normal voice. 'Why do you speak that way?' I repeated. 'Because it attracts attention,' was his obvious answer. He went on to add that he put 'sound systems together but things were tough at the moment'. Many here have fantasies of worthwhile and important vocations. He sounded reasonable and calm but just a little out of sync.

Throughout the city the 'Godots' push their carts, piled up with a symbolic home comprising tins, a few cups, broken radios, bicycle parts and sometimes a forlorn dog attached by a piece of string. One old gent even goes around on roller blades, stripped to the waist, with his long hair bound like a Buddhist priest. Opposite my motel a woman on the far side of the boardwalk stands and leans against a wall posing as a prostitute in her knee-length boots and mini skirt. Close up, however, she is a toothless hag and although she is by no means selling whatever she has got left of her wares she has a compulsion to stand from 7 a.m., all day long, in the same spot, year after year. She has reasonable legs and from a distance might attract the curiosity of an idle john who might make the journey only to be screamed at since this is her kick. She sleeps in a doorway.

After, like Halley's comet, I have circled the world a few times and have once more settled back in the asylum of Venice I know that she will still be standing there and at night I will hear the feverish scratchings at the garbage bins as the human rats of Venice make their nightly forage.

3
Shopping in the Santa Monica Mall

More from Godot-Land where those without sit and rot in the alleyways of Venice, sleep on the beach and raid the garbage bins in the morning, while we think of our obsessions and head for the temple where desires may be momentarily pacified – the Santa Monica Shopping Mall. Entering the vast emporium we almost float along myriad passageways, pausing here and there like fish nibbling at the mossy sides of rocks, sniffing in crevices, searching for that passive object that we can engulf, ingest into our being, like those sea sponges which trap little shrimps and slowly absorb them into their systems – thus we swallow down our compulsions. We are contented for a while until a new desire wells up that only a forage through the mall can satisfy.

We see things that suddenly we feel we can't do without, as if there was a deep longing, a hollow in the pit of the stomach which contained an unendurable hunger that can never be quelled. Then you try on something and perhaps it renews, remoulds, colours, gives you a new form, redefines who you are and adds another flavour to the palette of your personality. So you enter the vast mall perhaps to reconstruct, narrow your waist, heighten your length, brighten your dullness and each store sucks you into the maelstrom of decisions provoking you to change. What you cannot immediately achieve through the dazzling metamorphosis of fashion which can stylise your flaccid body, you may be forced to achieve by cutting, nipping, tightening, lifting, liposucking, slicing, tucking and so all the time the need is there to change for something better than yourself as if you were a piece of merchandise that you could never take back. The dark cave inside your soul is full of the snakes of anxieties that seethe and writhe and cannot be stilled. They will provoke you to compare yourself to everything that walks on the planet Earth and where the shortfall is between yourself and the fantasy that you covet, another snake will incubate in the fertile juices of your frustration. So change, pump iron, sweat your balls off on the treadmill looking like a zombie as one leg goes up and the other goes down in that rapid motion like you were a slave treading grapes, only there is nothing you are producing here except a moronic dazed expression that the repetitive stair climbing induces. So the body expands and the endorphins flow but as the outer muscles define themselves, striate, bifurcate, delineate and the stomach resembles a washboard or a pound of sausages the desire within increases, or the emptiness, like a balloon blown up with air. But there is the satisfaction when you see the new self emerge.

   To get to the toys of the mall you must go through an avenue of food, a veritable Scylla and Charybdis of culinary fantasy and chart the narrow reefs like Ulysses. You may look but not partake but even as the sirens behind the counter lift their heads and open their mouths and their breasts heave and their hands point to carnal lingual delicacies, you must try to forge ahead, breasting the waves of desire. For the first few days you may be able to do so with that English fortitude borne out of resistance

Shopping in the Santa Monica Mall

and abstinence but after a few more mouth-watering excursions you might linger, watching the delicate Oriental girl gently ladling the gravy on to the stir-fried beef, admire the deep but unreal bottle-green of the broccoli, smile at the defiant size of sandwiches that will be made to your own unique specification in a multiple array of combinations. One temptation will touch that special molecule of memory, that childhood taste and the button will be pressed that slows your journey through the isles of sensuality and gluttony. The seven deadly sins start here. Instead of choosing which café to visit, here the cafés wrap themselves round you as you walk and each smell and sight beckons, sends a wisp into your nostrils and a salivating colour to your brain. You have told yourself that it is only a roll of film that you require and that object was the motivation to visit the mall but under that objective what other distant cries made themselves heard from the deep pit. One day I was sorely tempted to taste (not having really breakfasted) that special fried egg and lean bacon sandwich and it was so hot and tasty and the egg was as yellow as a field of corn inside its toasted roll and the bacon crispy and frizzled. I am now a consumer in the hall of taste. I sit and may as well enjoy, having succumbed, and watch as others walk swiftly in but then slow down as if they were soldiers cut down by a fusillade of bullets, the bullets of temptations, fantasies and needs.

I watch the others who come in here to sit and sample and for whom the giant mall is a sanctuary, if not for the spiritual at least the physical, where we worship at the altar of cornucopia. Here we kneel in prayer before the god of Mammon and offer up our donations to the powerful one who WILL give us a piece of Heaven on this Earth rather than the one in the cold, draughty, empty church who will give us zilch except the thin satisfaction of having donated something to get a new window put in or the roof repaired. Here we GET!! Here we can be within reach of everything that might fill the great, empty, dark, vacant void where the soul has died. We can fill the painful emptiness and stave off the great and gnawing hunger with whatever that may be, either the latest baseball cap in satin with coloured stones that you simply must have or those real cool cowboy boots with pointed toes that will change your life. But the faces in the food hall have a pained expression as if their souls were caught in purgatory while their bellies are crawling over their belts like overflowing lava. Some look truly at peace though, while others look as if they had no friends, and no other place to go since the mall is friend to the lonely and isolated, a comrade to the weird and neuro, and is a paradigm for the America that says on the Statue of Liberty, 'Bring me your poor and oppressed'. The mall will embrace you all, distinguishes none and bars none as long as you offer the plastic tribute. They sit there as if this was their church of consumology where they will not be lectured, hectored, instructed and selected but wooed, loved, caressed and pampered and where friends you have never met before will say, 'And how are you today?' and smile at you and they may be the only ones who will talk to you all day and the only voices to crack the wall of silence and anyway it is so much FUN! But after the fun, what else? Like the tides you will withdraw into the bright, harsh, sunlit world outside and wait until hunger once more persuades you to visit.

Some faces look more in sync here than with the world outside since the food section is their particular pond and where they make their daily trip. Two elderly ladies who are identical middle-aged twins sit in their matching colours and hairstyles, happy that they can be part of this ebb and flow. They were content to be looked at in this vast hall of food since this was their theatre where their uniqueness might not go unnoticed. Here they are unselfconsciously nibbling their lunch as if to be identical in every way down to the tiny ringlets over their forehead, to their clothes, colour and make-up, and only in such a huge hall could they play to so many spectators.

'Is it fat free? No caffeine, no sodium, no sugar, no

cholesterol, no sweeteners, no additives, no oil, no tastes, no smoking, for Jesus Christ our Lord, Amen.'

There are those who shop but bring their houses with them, which would be difficult anywhere else but the mall is big enough for all and the homeless wheel their trolleys, their shopping carts filled with their worldly possessions, and queue for merely the cheap side portions, the hash browns or some toast. In the heat outside they push their carts along like Mother Courages circling the great cathedral of everlasting plenty where computers and giant 'dogs' are the daily hymn but they dare not come in at first and some never do. They circle like the undead in the outer rings of Dante's Inferno, and to the regular customers they appear like aliens from another world for that is the way of life in America and if your jaw does not have a firm strong-toothed grip on the American nipple, you will then be as a bug scrounging around for dung. Is that why there is such a strong belief in aliens since so many appear to be aliens already?

So these aliens who have crawled out of parks, from behind trucks, out of derelict rooms, from windswept beaches, parking lots and alleyways, walk zombie-like through the Santa Monica streets with a constant prayer on their lips for some small change but if you fail to acknowledge their prayer they will not be pained but bless you with a benediction of having a nice day, since they don't know when you might cross their paths again. A fat lady walks on crushed high-heeled shoes wearing a pink fitted wool dress that reveals and accentuates her wedges of fat yet it holds her together so she may imagine she presents a wholesome image of femininity while pushing the stigma of poverty and homelessness, her shopping trolley, as if it were a pram in which lay sleeping an adored child. Another alien sits by the pier with a card around his neck that announces his poverty and extreme dire state, 'Homeless and hungry', while another with a touch more inventiveness has written on his card, 'No home, no job, no kidding', thus investing a touch of humour to his role of pauper which helps us shoppers feel less guilty. These creatures are able to sit for hours in the same position and you notice them as you arrive at the mall and when you leave maybe a couple of hours later. You exit blinking in the raw sunlight backed by a cobalt-blue sky, picking the crumbs out of your teeth, and are suddenly reminded of their existence which is re-emphasised by the passage of time. One man with the 'cord' is still there, still sitting cross-legged. While these last two hours were full of Western-booted excitement, waterfalls of colour and confusions of taste ending in deep fulfilment, this man's lifestyle suffered extreme sensory deprivation. Thus whilst you giggled, chewed, masticated and stared at the female weightlifters on the TV while waiting for your bill, he was just waiting, and as you slurped your decaffeinated cappuccino he was still there, and so out of a feeling of deep compassion you dipped your hand into your pocket and paid him a dollar to numb the ache of your guilt.

4
Salome in Canterbury

First night over in a converted cinema splendidly recreated as a theatre with the added benefit of a panoramic stage. Thank God they didn't sacrifice it to the bingo god. Before the dress rehearsal, cast all come in cursing after trying to find a way into the Marlowe Theatre since the one-way system and the British predilection for indifferent signposting causes us to impersonate Theseus in the Maze, twisting this way and that and at last we find the one magic route. I have a theory about this lack of desire to clearly make signs. You come to a junction and there is no sign left or right – my theory is too laborious to go into now, but I felt it was rooted in the British inability or desire to communicate... When I arrive, I bump into the manager of the theatre who kindly proffers the news that the matinées are nearly zero at the moment but they might get ninety in if we're lucky! 'It's the exams, you see, they're all sitting exams.' I didn't know what he was on about at first since I imagined the theatre was for people of all ages and didn't realise how much the provinces have already neglected, abused, lost and destroyed their audiences until they have to rely on select 'groups'. So the idea of playing for ninety-plus in a theatre seating 1000 is not only a gloomy thought but a contemptible one in making a company act through a two-hour journey, to say nothing of the exhaustion of playing Herod twice in a day. An opera singer wouldn't dream of doing two shows in a day but most acting is now geared around undemanding rigours of naturalistic theatre, so producers and directors who don't have to get off their arses have few qualms about killing off actors eight times a week. John Dexter is quoted in his posthumous biography, as saying a great actor finds it impossible, if he or she is truly taking theatre to where it belongs (and that is at the gates of Hell!), to do it twice in one day. Good actors can, and do, by saving themselves and so the public is cheated. Do you think Kean or Irving would do two shows in one day? Never! Although Kean might do a curtain-raiser or Harlequin to show his dexterity. Only when Boucicault organised the theatre in the late nineteenth century did he introduce the matinée, and why not – as a playwright he didn't have to play it. I maintain that if the actor is pulling out all stops he will be maimed by doing two shows. It killed off Brando from his year's stint in *Streetcar* on Broadway and he never returned to the theatre, and poor Viv went potty.

It's an exhausting performance; we rehearse the entire show in the afternoon as we do once a week so that we might be prepared for the differing acoustics and since I am not in the first half I am able to watch and am still able to find it enchanting. The set arrived from Berlin as if on a magic carpet and the lights worked perfectly, and naturally the actors take it for granted, as they should, that someone has driven a huge pantechnicon through Europe from Brighton to Lisbon, Berlin to Canterbury. I am impressed since this is the first time I have toured with something that couldn't be packed into a few suitcases. After the dress rehearsal we drift along the main pedestrian arterial vein of tourist Canterbury. Twenty-five years ago I performed here in a pot-boiler called *Write Me a Murder*. Then at a later date I performed the messenger in the T. S. Eliot verse play *Murder in the Cathedral*, which was put out in the heyday of BBC TV drama when intelligence guided choice and the public was respected. The event of the week was the Wednesday Play and TV was fuelled by drama and epic themes. Alas, bygone days. Cyril Cusack played Thomas à Becket and during his big sermon Cyril fixed me with a basilisk stare and he said later that I had a good eye to help focus on during his large speeches, and I was proud of that and clung to him later like a fan when he drank his weird concoction of whisky and milk, although I had to disagree with him on his religious theories which were extremely right wing.

Now, thirty years later, I wander down what is now a pedestrian area festering with boutiques, hamburger joints, overpriced and indifferent hotels, souvenir shops and one good vegetarian café called Mungo into which I collapse with much relief and find the rest of the cast in there, since travelling actors have an innate sense to sniff out what is good for them. The street is also charming for its architectural bewilderment and the great mock-Tudor library sits in the centre opposite the County Hotel, famous for its terrible service but to which I will eventually escape from something infinitely worse. As I walk through the narrow thoroughfare past the beautiful canal that snakes its way through the city, I come across the great gaunt cathedral and view it suddenly through a side street as if by chance. It dominates the town with its Gothic splendour, awesome and magnificent, and all melts away before this majestic lady. The town seems to gather at its skirts, is fed by it, sucking like a thousand tiny runts as the great work of art draws the world to see it. Once I actually stayed in the cathedral precincts, when a local vicar let rooms to actors, and had to enter the locked gates with a pass key. The great door had a smaller door within it. I drift back to the theatre and recall a charming old tea shop right opposite the cathedral where you could sit and contemplate your life but now it's turned into an ice cream monster spewing out its pastel-coloured glutinous concoctions while in the window sits a stuffed animal with a red light on it. It's disgusting, rotten and hideous and of course faces the cathedral. Naturally it's patronised by thousands of screaming Euro-trash types wearing multicoloured track suits and completely oblivious to what they are seeing. They are totally absorbed by each other and shout, scream, push, eat, play and pay no real attention to what is around them. They cannot. They don't have the contemplative air with which to view this marvellous piece of history. They pour over it like locusts and then flee with hands clutching those evil red Coke cans and artificial ice cream.

I return to the theatre with a heart of lead to prepare, and since the stage door is mysteriously locked I can't get in. 'The stage doorman is off at 6 p.m.,' the box office kindly explains. I then go through the front after being given the number of the code for the various doors I must use. All very conducive, you see, to a sense of well-being for your night's performance. The foyer bar is lined with photos of actors who have graced this theatre. It is a grim rogue's gallery with whom you could cast all of Alan Ayckbourne's plays, solid middle-class, smiling down brightly, cheeks bunched and although there are some very good actors there I swiftly determine that my mug shall not be one of them. I hardly know a soul there anyway, except Vincent Spinetti who grins at me knowingly. I feel that by now we have come to the wrong place although it is a splendid theatre and well equipped. I examine the green room and read the posters of past triumphs. It is the Montague Burton of touring theatres: dollops of Agatha Christie (a sure sign of terminal recession), a bit of Kent Opera which is very worthy, but I do notice a *Hamlet* with Mark Rylance and cheer up again. My eye clings to that image. It is a good theatre for acoustics and a pin can be heard dropping. I go to my dressing room to prepare and notice a card inviting us afterwards for a drink with the 'Friends of the

Theatre'. I can only imagine what this may mean and ask our company manager to book a restaurant anyway for the cast so at least we can finish on a hearty note.

The performance receives polite laughter and some enthusiasm at the curtain call; the audience has done its best. The cheering, standing ovations we received in Lisbon and Berlin must be relegated to memory to warm us on cold winter evenings. After all, we are a more restrained nation, especially in the Tory hinterlands. The show is finished and I believe I put as much as I could into it. There is no 'feedback' from anyone and I drag my bones in to meet the 'Friends of the Theatre'. A woman shouts at me, 'WHAT WOULD YOU LIKE TO DRINK...BEER? OR A GLASS OF WINE?' My tongue cleaveth to the roof of my mouth. I actually can't speak. She repeats, 'I HEAR YOU LIKE BEER, DON'T YOU?' She seems to believe that she has discovered some secret vice, when in fact I *loathe* beer, I hate beer; the smell of it and the places that sell it, and I am not potty about the people who drink it. 'A glass of champagne would be nice.' They look a little crushed. After all I am still dragging vibrations of Herod with me, he lingers in the blood...it takes a while to de-tox...what's the big deal anyway. They seem to have received a wobbly but gamely accept the challenge with all the fortitude of an Anneka Rice contestant and go stomping off. At the bar a local weirdo journalist has a fixation in repeating the same question, amounting to how many ways she can say 'Why *Salome*? Why Oscar Wilde?' why this and why that and 'What do you think of Chekhov?' as if I was a machine at a fun fair that gives your weight. Having slipped inside my 'precinct' at the bar they think they are compelled to make a meal of it.

The challenger 'Friend' comes along to say that the champagne is warm and so I accept a vodka and tomato juice. I ask for another. The barmaid appears to have a problem with this order, engages in a tête-à-tête with her colleague and comes back and whines, 'You have to pay for this one.' So the

Friends treat us to strictly one drink, it would appear. We flee into the night leaving the Friends to each other and now needing some good fortune, *please*, we find the best Mexican restaurant in Britain. It's called Les Amis. The margaritas sting and the fajitas are bursting with flavour, and the manager welcomes us with a warmth I would have liked earlier. The company has become one animal with many feet and hands and there is much laughter, chat and satisfaction. I repair to my hotel, the Friar, and a very pretty room with a four-poster bed.

Breakfast

A group of gloomy tourists sit waiting for one waitress to run around. On a table behind me are the packets of cereals, dozens of them, and so inches from my ear I hear the customers struggling to open their mini-packets which seem to offer great resistance. Eventually the things ripped and the dry contents could be heard rattling their sparse flakes on to a bowl, sounding like nail filings. The waitress is absorbed in writing something on the counter which still has mounds of last night's unwashed glasses on it. I read my newspaper and wait. Eventually my tense stillness has sent over a vibe that a human is waiting for breakfast. It seems I have still these extraordinary powers, which I learnt from Houdini, of assuming invisibility. It seems to happen involuntarily, like an erection I imagine. She shunts her weary form over to me: 'WHAT ROOM NUMBER ARE YOU?' Now I am in the Army being drilled for info... I might have liked a 'Good morning' first, a 'What would you like?' or any form of civilised greeting but the poor thing has her conditioned patter worked out. I said, 'Let's not worry about that right now,' and then she rattled off the usual breakfast list which was seared in her and delivered like a satanic rite to the Devil. 'What about,' I ventured unadventurously, 'scrambled eggs on toasted brown?' 'Yer, okay.' I await my breakfast after a hard first night in the cavernous Marlowe Theatre and lift the teapot lid hoping not to see two soggy tea bags hanging by their strings like discarded Tampaxes but such hopes are in vain and the tasteless yuck, the symbol of British laziness, is there as feared, in all its disgusting glory. She comes with my deadly-pale scrambled eggs sitting atop some soggy toasted WHITE BREAD... but, I exclaimed, I did ask for the brown bread, to which she hastily pouted that they had run out. Meanwhile in the corner of my eye the fruit machine was flickering insanely like it was having a silent laugh. Nobody was going to put coins in it at 8 a.m. and so I expect it was to give the room a bit of character. I am in the middle of yob culture. I split and am determined to have a civilised breakfast without the flickering fruit machine and even – perish the thought – with *real* tea. I discover a branch of Liberty's here and Lo and behold! a beautiful tea room with chintzy curtains and real tea. I sat down and wept...

Later, refreshed and moved, I visited the cathedral, this miracle of man's superabundant genius. I strolled through the cloisters and on the ceiling were the small bosses that link the joins of the vaulting and instead of bosses were the faces of the builders who worked on the cathedral centuries ago and I suppose it was like seeing the faces of the actors in the bar at the Marlowe Theatre. We all like to leave behind a memento. I trailed behind one group since they were being informed by a guide who had the delivery of Alec McCowen and the same passion as when Alec performed the Gospel according to Saint Mark. He was a retired archbishop and under his tutelage the stones and stained glass of the cathedral came bounding to life. Just like the skill of a great actor.

Thursday, 17 June

Last night's show was very good except for a small blip in one speech which shows you can never take your brain for granted. A mild panic set in and then the ship righted itself. Applause stronger and more laughs. After washing off make-up, sat contemplating my hot pink washed face. Drifted into bar. Just a few stragglers from the audience. No feedback or comment. The bar exuded that dead feel of English pubs where the only sustenance is crisps, and so we sit and drink in two groups. I stroll back to the hotel across the road determined to make it before the last order for dinner or food, advertised at 10.30 p.m. But there is no way, I learn, that I will be served after ten. It seems incredible that I should have to point out to them that the signs on the menu and on the outside of their building state categorically 10.30 but the manager could only shrug and say they would have to change it. The mealy-mouthed obeisance by customers to such arrogantly indifferent behaviour is, I suppose, why they still get away with it. So instead I was able to wheedle a sandwich and a beer in my room. The dining room looked glum anyway and a few bored faces sat mordantly at the bar and the ubiquitous blinking machine sat there flashing obscenely like an electronic granny that you are forced to live with forever and which will never shut up. I have yet to see anyone use it as it blinks pathologically all day. I crawl up the musty bed-and-breakfast smell of the staircase and await my sandy.

Breakfast
They have bought a loaf of brown bread especially, I am informed before partaking of my breakfast, and I sit myself far away from the ritual of the tearing mini-packets of cereal. I order eggs on toast again and tea and it actually tastes good, and Lo and behold! the machine has not been switched on yet. A woman comes down to breakfast and starts unzipping her anorak which crackles with the rubberised synthetic junk it is made from and then she tears open a packet with more crackles. She appears to be a lone voyager and wears the distinct mien of someone who knows that their lot in life is to be unloved but will hope to navigate the day without too much

abuse from the world. Under her anorak she reveals one of these multicoloured dresses with giant flowers all over it and it falls shapelessly over her shapeless body. However, this kind of dress is much beloved among the British middle class, a kind of over-bright cotton thing with gardens growing all over it. The hair is usually short and curled and silver-grey and they can be seen in all the shopping centres, particularly Waitrose. They look healthy and totally celibate, even a little priestly. This one in the breakfast room is also wearing trainers for some sensible walking and is deeply appreciative of everything the sullen waitress brings. So when she requests a little Cheddar cheese, its arrival is celebrated with benedictions of 'You're very kind,' like she was the Elephant Woman and has just discovered the milk of human kindness after years in a cage as a side-show. I keep turning my head in disbelief that the electronic moron is dead! I'm surprised that the landlord doesn't keep his toy flickering all night so its undulating shimmer might be seen from the windows.

I return to my four-poster room and stare idly out of the window facing the theatre where the poster of *Salome* is facing another one advertising a pirate show. People seem to be ambling along in a kind of vacant purposefulness like they might be extras in the TV series *The Prisoner*. Shall I leave? Go into the country? Commute to London? To my shock I realise I have only been here two nights and it feels already like a month. I go downstairs and will drive myself to Whitstable and walk along the sea-front. As I hand in my room key I see that the blinking maniac is performing its epileptic dance again. I decide to calmly question the lady who works there. 'Is it really necessary to have that thing on when people are having breakfast? Isn't it a wee bit antisocial having it blinking in your eyes telling you to spend money?' She looks at me as if I had just left the pages of Edgar Allen Poe, since for her these things are a fact of life, like onion-flavoured crisps and sliced white bread, condoms and birth pills. Then came her mantra: 'I HAVE

TO SWITCH IT ON 'CAUSE THE MANAGER ASKS ME TO.' There was no desire to communicate on the simplest of human levels, no desire to confront the essence of what I was saying like 'Do you think it bothers people or why?' No, she had shut off all dialogue and repeated her mechanical lobotomised response – the authority of the manager telling her to...

Friday, 18 June
The theatre may be attracting and word getting round since a few 'Bravos' rang out last night and warm enthusiasm from the tiny matinée audience. A whole skewer of young girls come to the stage door and are from the local college... the enthusiasm of women. They all streamed in clutching their programmes and posters to sign. There seem to be a lot of coughers out there this afternoon. The kind of people who help to destroy your carefully built-up atmosphere with a well-timed cough detonated right in the middle of your speech when you have devoted your energy to weaving a spell, working on the minds of the audience, leaking vital psychic fluids into the atmosphere and then hhhhrrrrph! COFF, COFF! Like they were at home watching a video.

I left the fruit machine hotel yesterday after I came down at 7.30 and found it blinking its stupid life away. It seemed to symbolise by now the hotel and its occupants. I told her to switch the blasted thing off and she reluctantly switches it off as if I were some kind of loony and not *these* people who turn such a thing on at 7.30 a.m. No, THAT is sensible. 'I'll switch it off for some peace of mind until you've finished breakfast.' I tried this time to calmly reason with her since this mound of flesh is surely capable of reason and not just a product of ghastly Canterbury conditioning that thinks all people are tourists to be sucked as they wander down this long pedestrian street running the gauntlet of little shops and nasty cafés. She goes into her favourite hit – 'the manager tells me' syndrome. Surely, I reason, nobody can want to play the machine at 7.30 in the morning when eating their breakfast, and at the beginning of a new day. You don't really want to jump out of bed and say, 'Whoopee, let's get on the fruit machine.' Of course I know this hotel is still a pub and nowadays these machines can be seen defacing nearly every hostelry in the land, acting like some kind of mechanical prostitute that promises more than it gives and whom the manager or landlord pimps from, although, unlike the machine, some prostitutes do give value. Now the machine has grown in my mind to not only a symbol of Britain but an example of dissolution and decay. Of pubs too lazy and stupid to make money by their skills as chefs or barmen, so they have to drag in machines to make ends meet since all they can do is pull pints and take the tops off bottles. Her waxen expression changed not a jot as I tried valiantly to kindle some spark of human response. 'Surely,' I repeated, 'no one wishes to gamble at breakfast when most of your breakfast eaters wrestling with their packets of All-Bran seem to be serious cathedral groupies wearing sensible shoes and boning up on twelfth-century England.' 'Well,' she added, 'They start using the machine at ten, but I go off before ten so I have to switch it on before I go off.' I see. What she obviously tried to convey is that they are open for booze at 10 a.m. and so one assumes the machine comes to life then, to go with drinking, smoking and eating vinegar crisps.

The week drifted by. *Eric the Viking* was the next show following us in. I seemed to wander up and down this sluggish river of a street as if one couldn't easily escape its current. The human flotsam drifted down with the tide like a slow-moving river gathering all junk ready to carry it away to the sea and expel it into the endless ocean but before it does it is sucked back up again. Shell-suited families sucking on pastel ice creams wend their way down clinging to silver helium balloons shaped like dinosaurs and one of these was actually seen walking round the cathedral past the Black Knight.

Eventually I left my drab digs since it was impossible to take the sourness that emanates from negative human beings, and asked for my bill and it appears they had charged me £22 for one 28-minute call to London since it seems that hotels are legally permitted to interfere with BT's units and fiddle. And BT allows this and what this means is that without your knowledge, and with full co-operation from your kindly Telecom, your hotel can make whatever it likes, and in this case (after checking the unit price with British Telecom) I found that even at peak time my call would have been no more than £2.50, so they were marking up 1000 per cent. Normally a foreign guest, or any guest, does not query such items. It might have been better to be mugged since then you do have a chance. When I did query the bill they reduced it immediately with no apology but with the rider 'It's on units, you see' as if this piece of technological info masked their blatant thieving. I happily moved into the smarter County Hotel where I was immediately refused just coffee at 12 p.m. since it was mandatory that you ate! A gloomy hatchet-faced waitress delivered her sermon with appropriate venom.

We had a good last night at the theatre and two shows that day. Exhausted but euphoric I crawled to the bar where a glass of water was thrown at me by a neurotic fan who felt he was being ignored, and then ran out like a furtive rat. I was not sorry to see the end of Canterbury.

5
Salome in Chicago

Saturday, 14 October

Yesterday on Friday the 13th gave a good performance; in fact, one of the best of the run since I tried less, much less after Kirsten hinted that a little would be more... So after an empty afternoon of cappuccino and spring rolls, the theatre. I'm early since nobody told me it's 8 p.m. tonight instead of 7.30. It's warm and I sit around in the dressing room learning *De Profundis* as a kind of meditation but then I run a little of the play, the last big speeches, and feel better for it. Our Irish musician, Roger, comes in and practises for a while and plays fast and cleverly. I drift around trying to make the minutes dissolve of their own accord. I stand outside in the twilight warmth, then learn a few more lines from *De Profundis* and it sticks more in my mind, and have a fantasy about learning the whole piece for a one-man show but it's unlikely... I go back to my room and I hear the actors return and continue learning. Tonight we have a reception after the show and we are looking forward to being wined and dined.

I put make-up on and it spreads easily without the smudges

the heat usually causes but I am ready too early and Cathy my dresser keeps coming in and is sent away again since I don't want the waistcoat and coat on *just* yet. I keep redoing my lips... I think I will act more with them tonight. I purse my repainted lips and against my white face they seem like two snakes. As a last resort I read *Premiere* movie magazine and learn about the antics of the idiots of Hollywood and yet again there is this picture of an agent called Mike Ovitz who is utterly irrelevant but in the world of arse-licking the rich and the famous, he is never far from the newspapers. Who cares? Eventually I enter and am determined to do less and be cooler, thinner...

I walk along the corridor having shaved my head down to the sandpaper which helps the white make-up go smoothly over. Cathy listens to my latest bug and advises... I decide to fight... As I enter I actually feel an element of fight in my genes. Carmen Du Sautoy is waiting in the semi-darkness at the side of the stage and we have the few words we exchange daily. She's exhausted she says from... SHOPPING! Just that, shopping. No male would ever admit this but on the other hand it is not a bad way to get involved in another kind of theatre. It can be quite dramatic, as I have learned to my bitter cost. I get on the stage and take the voice down a bit and by this I am refining and selecting. It is one of my better shows and I am happy tonight, so happy. My champagne and orange juice waiteth for me and I wash my hot head under the cold running tap.

It's washed off. I dry vigorously and stare at my newborn self. Reborn out of the ashes of the old performance. A trial of fire. Every night fear, pain and immense concentration and at the end of all endeavours the ritual has been enacted and you're free and off the hot seat until the next night. Cathy collects my costume and says as usual that it seemed to go well. The house cheered as I came on for my curtain call which they didn't always for my Coriolanus. Carmen says the house was good tonight when really she means we played better. Now we are invited to this looked-forward-to reception after the show and Susan Lipman (the producer) takes me round. She is wearing a double-breasted pinstripe suit and wraps me in compliments and bundles me upstairs to meet her patrons. The show went up a bit late to accommodate them since they were having a pre-show dinner and now after the show they are having dessert which we have been invited to share. So they are enticed to see us with treats before and after, with us in the middle as the entrée. We enter a darkened room where a crowd of people are waiting expectantly and noshing on tiramisu and strawberries dipped in chocolate. Susan asks if she can announce me which she does as if I were a guest in one of those old movies being announced by the maître'd... The small crowd splatter me with applause and then stop as I modestly pretend to be a guttersnipe, grateful to be picked up by the society's affection. Shy, humble and terribly grateful. That is the traditional stance. After all, they have brought you over. An elderly couple are thrust at me and I wait while they pat me with compliments and scratch my ears. Susan asks what I would like to imbibe and since I am in Chicago I fancy a vodka with cranberry but orange will do. She brings me back a tacky Yankee champagne in a plastic wine glass. Various types swan up to me making an assortment of pleasant sounds and meanwhile the cast have wandered in, their eyes on stalks for food since they seldom eat before a show and once offstage are like wolves off a tether, ready to devour anything in sight both on a plate or on two legs: after a show you have twenty hours to recover from any indulgences. They are greeted with these pathetic chocolate strawberries being circulated as if they either were rare treats or have been over-ordered. Since one has a craving for real food, the strawberries with shitty-looking arses become even more repellent.

More faces drip in and out, offering hands that are usually a little greasy and by now the back of your trousers becomes a cloth you use to surreptitiously wipe your hand on. Now I have found the bar and ordered my precious vodka and orange and have lit a cigarette and drift around making a beeline for the younger and more voluptuous members of the staff, one of whom is already surrounded by a posse of English actor bees. At last the party dissolves and we all head to the much desired, needed and looked-forward-to dinner but alas as we drive around with our limited knowledge of Chicago we realise that little is open and while the 'patrons' had stuffed themselves like pigs we were kept behind and permitted only to indulge in their revolting desserts which nobody much wanted and now we were even denied a grand nosh-up in a Chicago watering hole. Eventually we slid into a gigantic diner that was just closing and stuffed ourselves rotten on fast food junk hovered over by a fat waitress who kept bellowing how many minutes we had left but we appreciated the humour since she was at least vintage. The beautiful girl from the reception came with a man friend. Her name was Elise and she was not only highly attractive but blessed with a divine disposition... I crashed out in the Hotel Whitehall which is the very best, cosiest and most charming hotel I have stayed at in America and slept like the dead.

6
Salome in New York: The Last Performance

Monday, 23 October

It was grey yesterday when I got up and the day was fraught with angst for the previous night's party or celebration and this caused the matinée to be pure hell beforehand. The wait before I came on, waiting for Salome to say her lines, was terrible. It seems as if I have heard them forever. I wait. Cathy the dresser waits... Is it time to put my waistcoat on? Cathy enters. I stand up. The make-up is already flaking. It is not adhering to the overheated skull... heating up as the blood boils in anxiety. Before the matinée I floated downstairs to check casually who'd like to come out for a meal after the show to feast our last night in New York, since for some reason it seems terribly important to me. This is after all a once-in-a-lifetime. I mean, it's NEW YORK! But when I go on stage I wish to wipe it out of my computer since it is sending the wrong signals, worming their way into my brain which is programmed for *Salome*, so while I, as Herod, am talking about 'the moon', I am also thinking about restaurants! So I decided to cancel the damned celebration and leave my brain clear and focused. I will eat instead with a couple of friends who happen to be here in New York but the core of me wishes to be with my team, the actors, and let them all meet each other. Because of my mood the matinée has none of the delightful fooling that usually makes the two shows easier to accomplish. Now it is hard work and, like my make-up, the lines are on a slippery sweaty slope. The make-up finally stays on like crumbling plaster over a damp wall of flesh. After the matinée, relief... for a couple of hours.

In the afternoon it was raining when I arrived and pelting sheets of rain plastered the windshield, soaking me just between car and stage door. I arrive hoping for a batch of messages... some people... letters... anything to dull the expectation of inevitability... the task ahead, to be always there... up, exciting, dynamic, bold, furious, awesome, clever, inventive and yet now feeling empty, dead, cold, fearful, anxious, hopeful, dread. So a few messages to gnaw on and to show that I LIVE OUTSIDE THIS PLAY. I HAVE SOME EXISTENCE OUTSIDE HEROD. When performing sometimes that's all there is: the wait, the passing of hours before the moment; that everything you do that day is determined by that moment; that you cannot do something that may affect that moment; that even a plan after the show may affect the MOMENT.

A friend coming though is good. It makes one a bit edgy but once on, the edginess turns to energy and the nerves light up the body and you become oblivious to pain as you climb inside your character. The extra plug of energy is like a faggot thrown on the fire: you heighten an inflection; a gesture, a suggestion outside the text which brings a laugh of appreciation. The laughter shores up the character and helps glue the concept together. The next night you miss the laugh since the confidence was lacking to fire at that split second when the target was in your sights and you missed! It fills you with dread. Is your timing off and why? Your skills are draining out like a car running on reserve. Is your mind going? Is your spirit elsewhere? The absence of the laugh means there is a hole in the fabric. The laugh was *always* there since humans are so alike that each night the laugh comes and with it a special flavour, a knowing sound, a raised eyebrow sound. But tonight it didn't come. Maybe somebody stole it. Maybe the Queen Herodias or a member of the chorus shifted suddenly, drawing attention away. But that afternoon it came, perhaps not quite so solidly but definitely there. I had waited in the wings to go, thinking about dinner with friends at the St Regis or celebrating with the cast at Café America, a vast giant concrete hangar of a building. I imagined the cast liking this. It's bold, daring, powerful and an apt symbol of a nation that prides itself on gargantuan enterprises and has fulfilled itself in this huge and fantastic café. A giant bar, one of the largest I have seen, stretched out at the back like an altar. The faces line up behind it as if they were judges sitting at some vast bench and each nursing their drink. The judges of booze.

After the matinée, the relief: a good, a very good response, cheers and bravos. I managed not only to fake the emotion but actually to get through it with a spit of petrol and a mind leaking oil from its overheated brain. I washed off under the tap. I have a reprieve. Our touring manager comes back and tries to relieve me of the curse and take the problem out of my head, even making a funny gesture of extricating it out like those so-called healers drawing the evil spirits out of the brain. 'Don't worry,' she says. 'We'll do it in Madrid... early rise for everyone to catch the plane, actors tired etc... champagne in the corridor!' But, I thought, but *we're in New York*! So I took my assistant Graeme with his angelic face and clear blue eyes for a walk to Juniors, one of my favourite delis on the planet Earth. I walk in the afternoon air feeling light like I just did a rehearsal and I can go again easily. We enter Juniors and grab a booth. We share a pastrami sandwich which arrived – a small landslide of beef ridiculously topped by a slice of bread. In order to eat it you have to grab it with both hands and crush it until your fingers are knuckle deep in greasy pastrami and at the same time open your jaws like a shark. So now we share it out ordering more rye bread and making more sandwiches since Reginald, another member of the company, has arrived. I love the atmosphere of Juniors, which is carefree, large, abundant and overflowing.

Then, having some time, we walked round Brooklyn which was alive with Saturday shoppers and we felt like privileged invisible beings from another planet observing the strange Earthlings. We entered a store full of young blacks trying on big baggy pants and hooded jackets. We moved eagerly inside the stream of young black energy and became part of Saturday Night USA. The last shopping fling before the excited, exhausted buyers traipse home with their booty through the chilled Brooklyn evening air. We walked back and the rain had cleared and cleansed the atmosphere which now hung electrically charged.

We entered the stage door. The play again! Tried juggling with three coloured balls, a little present from a fellow actor in the last film I did which was one of the worst experiences of all time and predictably turned out to be the worst movie ever made. I like the fact that I can now juggle, a little something I never thought I could ever do but somehow I have learned the system! Then made up for the second show but this time less sweaty underneath and my face looked no more like a flaking wall. I anticipated dinner after with my mates at the St Regis Hotel where one of them is staying. I imagined drinks beforehand downstairs in the theatre corridor; freedom, actors' smiles, relief, pleasure, that's fine. Then the St Regis Hotel, a beautiful bar. The need to be paid back for all this nervous sacrifice is intense in me. Just to return to my hotel room. Anathema, horror, sadness, pain. The open wound that feeds the audience must be replenished. During the second performance the little gnawing returns. When I visited the actors after the matinée they all said, 'But we *wanted* to do something after.' 'It's booked anyway,' I said. 'It's booked – Café America – so you can all go or whoever wants to.' I was now determined not to be Mum anymore and looked forward to my dinner with Ray and Tony at the St Regis. I don't wish to turn up at Café America with my friends and have to wait and wait for the cast to dribble in. I have suffered enough. And so it still hovered like a small dark cloud over my head which occasionally rained hot showers of acid over my skull.

But we got through. We did, not with great feelings, but we fought. The fearless, ruthless playful delivery lost a little of its velocity, its punch, but I crawled between the barbed wire and the minefields by giving myself stern injunctions to 'DO IT!... PERFORM... KNOCK THEM OUT.' Hoping against hope that these instructions would tap little spurts of energy or adrenalin or scrotonin or testosterone, to seep into my system. A thought must affect your body chemically, we know that unconsciously, and so I battled through. The joy when I finished that long bejewelled tirade of temptation was overwhelming since I was virtually done. I finished that hard, difficult, beautiful speech and waited in a joyous, free, relaxed, calm and purged state having shot my bolt and drifted off whilst Salome makes her final powerful dirge to the lifeless head that she kisses. I am sitting quietly in the semi-darkness while Peter Brennan expertly performs the execution. I intone my last lines, the last lines of the New York season, the last lines I will say on the stage in 1995, maybe the last time I will ever do this play again, and after 230 performances the last one. Maybe. 'Kill that woman!' The chorus turn to kill Salome and the lights slowly fade. At this moment I am the happiest I could be: perfect, endless, bliss. I stand stage right in the wings and hear the house erupt into cheers, bravos, claps, stamps, whistles and shouts. It is the end of Brooklyn and of our stay in America.

We go downstairs after we've washed off and drink

champagne and I am on the look-out for my friend but of course he doesn't turn up. So the St Regis is off. Director Tony Kaye, my recent friend, comes with a model so tall her head scrapes the clouds. Some of the actors say, 'Are you going to Café America?' Every actor needs a dream after their work, particularly me, and one of my dreams has just shattered. We all need something that gives life after the stage, something that is not fixed like a play, something that is improvised, something when you don't know what is happening next. Since I see my friend is not here I say, 'Yes, yes.' I am going now to Café America with Tony Kaye and the female skyscraper. YES. The cast will join me there.

We all assemble at the stage door but the bus hired for the actors won't take them five minutes or so out of his way and drop them off. 'No,' he says, he's paid to go to the hotel only. A fat lady on the staff says proudly, 'That's America!' She kept repeating her homily like she was farting a can of baked beans and this was her answer for stiffness, indifference and thuggish behaviour. 'THAT'S AMERICA.' Yessir, a real 'ornery bunch of critters. However, the cast leapt off at the Bowery, jumped in a cab and met us at the great palace of cuisine – Café America. I sat and waited at the giant altar and was baptised in vodka and cranberry juice. A few minutes later they all rolled in. I waved from the great bar to the figures in the distance. They came and were indeed amazed and looked in wonder and in awe at the splendour of capitalist America. We were all together minus a few odd bods and we sat and celebrated our last night in New York and this is precisely what I had *wanted* us to do. To be together on this special night and toast the end of our run in this city. I wanted this very much. I was extraordinarily happy. In fact, as Herod says in the play, I have never been so happy...

7
Rascals Deli Miami

172nd St Miami

As usual there is the fluttering of people going in and out of this large institution since these ancient Jewish delis are gathering places for the old Jewish world, so now I could see the odd old crapper shuffling along, reluctant to lift a foot even an inch off the floor. He scrapes his slow way as if he was sanding it and I can hear the raspy sound long after he has passed me. I approach and see that there is a group queuing at the door although it is only mid-afternoon and judging by their advanced age you might believe that they were waiting for attention outside a hospital. Now I can observe a constant coming and going from doors situated on opposite sides of the single-storey building, the restaurant symbolising the human body since you enter at one end and exit by the other. Squeezing the metaphor even more a cash desk is situated at the exit: therefore your vital monetary nutrition is extracted from you before you are evacuated. Near the mouth where I stand and wait are two lines, one for tables and one for the very large counter. Most people are opting for tables and booths where they can face each other and yack. The mouth is slowly swallowing the long tongue of the queue and eventually I am deposited in the huge stomach of the building. There are two huge rooms seemingly full of people happily munching away and a steady babble fills the air.

At the head of the queue stands an elderly female MD who occasionally strides up and down like a sentinel as if her life had reached a point of no return and is thus condemned for ever to parade the Isles of Deli. Her face seems to be at the apotheosis of magnificent decadence and reminds one of an aged crocodile, mouth open as if she were in the middle of some abstract conundrum or pained by a decision of overwhelming magnitude when actually all she is trying to do is breathe. Arthritis has curved her spine and placed an envious mountain on her back, and her hips seem to be rusted as she strides with a stiff but purposeful gait, yet on the brink of disintegrating into dust like a mummy exposed to air for the first time in 3000 years. But this Jewish mummy by the effect of an iron will forces those molecules to grip each other. Her fingers are bejewelled believing this adds adamantine solidity and her earrings are long, gross and could be called Jewish-Gothic. Her lips are a crude slash of red and her glasses are as huge as they can be with those handles that look as if they are worn upside-down. There is a marvellous corruption of all human culture in this woman and one feels that all the influences of the Middle East, Europe and even America have flowed together to spawn her. She sadly looks like a fascinating junk room of Western civilisation and yet what defines her character is an intense Jewishness, the full flowering of the ghetto. She is one of the many whom centuries of confined environments have interbred; a slender, attenuated and hawkish creature whose nerve centres are spun out to receive the finest vibrations. Her features seem to be made with the thinnest paste and yet her dark eyes glow with an indomitable will to live. Ageing has not given her the dignity of some equivalent gentile lady who with watery blue eyes and pinkened cheeks can waddle to the church bazaar in her grandmotherly way. No, this is Dracula, dragon, Babylonia and anxiety taken to stress levels that would kill most people. She wears a satin trouser suit and her stage is the grease-sticky floor of Rascals where corned beef is sliced by the ton each year and the munching millions return to the solace of 'love food'.

I have never in my life seen so many old people in one restaurant or one place. It is a sanctuary for the elders but more than that it is a graveyard, the grey ones' meeting place, almost a wake for their youth. For some reason the old Miami Jews don't seem to age as gracefully as their gentile cousins since they have a compulsive need to beautify themselves beyond the grave: hair is tinted a purply lavender or a straw-stiff blonde, the same colour I recall my poor mother dyeing her hair for so many years until it resembled tufts of grass but one day she gave up the habit and it turned into a dignified silver. Is it the Eastern, Polish, Russian influence that impels Jewish women to retain the vestiges of youth even within the ravages of age or did the squalid life in the teeming East Ends of cities demand that you be attractive? Was the fear of being left, unwanted of such unthinkable dread that the rouge, lipstick and dye became the allies of the housewife? The intensity of ghetto life drove the young woman to compete with her sisters with feverish desperation and even in the ghetto of Rascals the aged seem bent over and crippled, crushed beneath the weight of illness and woe. It is still the East Side of New York and the East End of London with a hairdresser on every corner. If you cannot alter your fate or environment at least you can make a masterpiece of your face.

Since I am alone I am seated by the great Jewish crow and find myself in the centre of the counter which is oval shaped. On my right is a strong-looking but weathered Jewish man with dyed hair sitting with his wife – he looks Russian – and on my left are two men in their seventies who still have a vitality beyond their years; a vitality of the pill, perhaps, since their faces are already turning a parchmenty white. I order a corned beef sandwich which is my rare indulgence, and ordered only in delis. The man on my right finds his corned beef sandwich rather large and as I crunch on the free bowl of pickles I sneak a look and observe him scoop out, using his finger and thumb, excess slabs of the meat and plonk it on his wife's plate whom he obviously has typecast as a human garbage disposal unit. Suddenly the meat looks obscene, the crude gesture defiling what in the sandwich looked respectable now looks raped with slovenly indifference. However, since she has been a garbage bin all her life the woman accepts the offering and immediately scoops it into her mouth without attempting to dignify it between two slices of rye. I carry on crunching from the mound of pickles in the aluminium bowl.

The queue for the tables is still long and from my barstool I can examine all the elders who are all grateful that another day has been blessed unto them and they can eat *kosher* deli. There are one or two younger ones and some middle-aged and the rest are elderly but an intense elderly that only a Jew pickled in angst, anguish, despair, *gavalt*, dread, can have. A face of no surprises and 'I have heard and seen it all!' So here is undiluted age, heavy age, age that has grown up in the shade, in dusty cities, the cholesterol overkill of chicken soup and meatballs, on work and more work, compulsive and debilitating work and on the guilt that is the legacy of a hounded soul. Guilt for pleasure when the world is full of hells. Guilt for living and guilt for sex, guilt for not making your children *menschen*. But the guilt is too strong to take and must be diluted with humour and humour is also the antidote of guilt, the humour of death, the humour of the gallows. *'I want to be buried under the pavement of Bloomingdales so that I know my wife will visit my grave three times a week!'*

The sandwich arrives and is excellent and the staff are all clean-looking, alert, middle-aged, and with a splattering of blacks. Traditionally blacks are seen in a way to be like Jews, emotional, overcooked Jews perhaps, big bosomy Jews and comfortable to be with, hence their love of *kosher* deli. The man on my right, the meat picker, lets out an involuntary belch, not huge but he quickly says, 'Excuse me.' I cannot help but visualise the home: the squashed sofa where for years he sits in the afternoon watching basketball, emitting an occasional belch which sends his wife scurrying to the cupboard to get a pill for his ulcers. A terrible familiarity reigns whereby all is permissible when the preservation of dignity is no longer an obligation since for whom does one have to be dignified? The inhibiting filters that held up the gunge have long since rusted and what is left is unspeakable and sadly incontinent. Because there is no pain to which the Jew has not been exposed, by knowledge if not directly, by osmosis, by empathy, by sympathy, by identification, and no pain has been too great, no humiliation too unspeakable, so the horror might leave one with an occasional *indifference to niceties*. Or, if not that, to the requisite codes of conduct that are deemed to be acceptable in polite society.

So, '*Eat darling. Enjoy!*'

8
One-night Stand Darlington

For some insane reason which I cannot fathom, my return ticket, First Class on a 2½ hour journey to Darlington, is £160. For the same money I could fly to Paris. The First Class is 25 per cent full. Through some crackling speakers a British Rail voice announces itself: 'My nime is Johnny and oim your buffet car attendant. We have pizza, hamburgers, etc.,' while in the background, as if to give credence to his claims, we hear the crashing of cutlery. The faces in the compartment break into smiles and giggles as if this is *so* British, amateurish and a bit tacky.

I was on my way to Darlington to perform *One Man* as part of my mini-tour of Britain. Tonight the show will start at 5.45 since it is the World Cup night. Without sounding too supercilious or like a snotty, arrogant, culture freak, I would have thought that a football match, even a World Cup, would affect one fan in a hundred as far as the taste of my public's concerned. Unlike Chekhovians, Barbicanians and Ayckbournians, Berkovian audiences have certain priorities and are far too intelligent to deny themselves the higher cultural input of *One Man* compared to watching what seems to be the same match each week played on telly. Anyway, I like the idea of people living and dying for their art, both punters and performers, and that it should be an event anticipated for weeks, queued for in discomfort for hours (preferably overnight) and that you will remember for the rest of your life. Now, can you compare that to a totally forgettable match on the telly whose only real excitement is the identification the audience puts into their 'team'? No, I cannot be shared with that. Nevertheless, just in case there are those who might be so tempted or divided, the administrator has decided to go up at 5.45 p.m.

I went to the buffet where Johnny was serving the sandies and was informed that they had run out of sandwiches until we get to York. There was hardly anybody using the buffet but they had sold out and so I took my muddy-tasting coffee back to my First Class, over-priced seat, which gives you no First Class service, as you would get on a plane.

Eventually we slid into Darlington. There is something unique about British northern towns on a Sunday. A deathly pall hangs over the station, which seems always to be situated in some depressing, low rent, industrial area surrounded by the faceless brick walls of some bottling plant or factory fallen into disuse. Acres of brick wherever you look. Some of the stations I passed hadn't been painted for so long their colours had almost faded, just retaining a glimmer, like a TV set when you have turned the colour down but not quite off. We are met by a jaunty little chap who strides along the platform with a seaman's sideways gait and has an inch of dead roll-up stuck in his mouth. We look for a trolley for Mark's (my musician) equipment.

Eventually and materialising out of a seemingly endless horizon of brick, a human being in the shape of Paul, my company manager/lighting designer, strides over to greet me. 'It's not so bad,' he says, 'when you get past this bit,' as we walk past more large brick edifices and completely deserted streets, like a town after the plague. We walk past the arena where I shall be pouring out copious amounts of sweat in three hours, the Civic Theatre. It's in the middle of its thriller season, a massive dose of Agatha Christie in weekly dollops. The theatre looks bleak, deserted and sad, a kind of potential victim just able to hold off the virus of bingo from claiming it. Now we come to the new complex of more bricks, but this time in orange and yellow and in which my hotel is situated.

On the walk my eyes gratefully took in a quick-flowing, shallow stream with green Ophelia-like weeds pulled back like hair. My Hôtel du Morgue sits waiting for its guests. As I enter – the familiar smell of synthetic carpets, cleaning fluid and old coffee mixed with 'fresh air' – my heart seems to sink deeper into its chest the way a frightened puppy will nuzzle into its protector.

There is something so fundamentally depressing about the British provinces that at first you suffer with your normally attuned senses but eventually you learn to temporarily lobotomise them in order not to scream with the pain of sensory deprivation. Two old silverhairs are sitting in the death lounge, nursing cans of something. I am not greeted with anything but 'Do you want a morning paper or an alarm call?' No 'Welcome to our hotel and I hope you will enjoy our pleasant sanctuary.' A robot could emit more warmth. In my room I can scarcely breathe but the reason I am here is to perform *One Man* and I try to summon up the will and excitement this should generate. But depression has now sucked the energy out of my legs so I collapse fully clothed on to my bed with my shoes on, not even having the will to pull them off. Eventually I drag my numbed body over to the window which sadistically looks out on to a gravel-lined roof supporting large metal pipes. In the distance a church steeple reminds me that there must be some form of human civilisation nearby and I suck some relief out of that.

I emerge in the lounge for some tea before my warm-up. I request this from the girl in the reception and this arrives fairly promptly.

The two grey-haired old ladies have gone but two twisted empty cans once containing fizz stand on the table opposite. A girl serves me the tea and when I ask if she has any sandwiches she repeats the word 'Sandwich?' in a slightly worried way that tempts me to believe that this particular form of eating is still unusual here. So I gently say, 'You know what I mean by sandwich?' 'Oh we have sandwiches but only on room service.' Did this mean I had to go all the way up to my room to be allowed to eat it. Obviously not, it was just a reflex action, and she brings a menu. The contents of the sandwiches are exactly the same as those on British Rail except *they* had run out until York.

Twenty minutes later I am still staring at the menu which says tuna fish and cucumber: £1.85. Although the waitress has been here twice now and there is no one in the room except me, the two empty cans opposite still stand there. With the leisure I have at my disposal I am able to study them. One is Coke and the other is Lucozade and they remain in the middle of the table, in this first-class hotel, like some kind of Warhol exhibit. Still nobody takes my order for my room service sandy and so eventually I rise and walk a few steps to the reception where two girls have been nattering.

B: I have sat here for a half hour studying a menu... any reason for this? I only request a sandwich.
REC: Well, we're really closed for food at the moment but if you're a resident we can order it for you.
B: But you know I'm a resident, you just signed me in.
REC: Oh, no, it's alright it's just that we're normally closed but we can get it for you because you're a resident...

This kind of crazy talk went on for a few minutes and I sat down again and resolved never to go north of London for the rest of my life.

This place is sourly reminding me of our tour last year to Nottingham and Birmingham when the whole company went down with a fit of depression. The last night in the rep theatre after a cheering house for *Salome* not one person came back to say even goodbye, let alone share a farewell drink. We contrasted this with our European trip, where at each theatre we were greeted as if we were of importance to them. These thoughts came flooding back here in this grim lounge. Still the time is passing nicely until my warm-up.

Another twenty minutes pass and I begin to wonder if I had really ordered my sandy or was it just in my mind and never materialised into speech. Or did the order get lost in the Socratic dialogue about being a resident and room service and all the rest of the junk language they are programmed to abuse you with. I am assured that the sandwich has been ordered and that Kathy was doing it. Eureka! It arrives smothered in the celebratory confetti of British crisps but it actually tastes good. Chewing happily I allow my eyes to wander out of the window of the lounge, where I can view a tunnel and two shops boarded up with 'To Let' signs.

According to Einstein everything is based on his theory of relativity and so while this applies to movement it can also apply to living: if you have just come out of prison you might find this paradise, equally if you had escaped from Bosnia. But if you have the normal human desire to witness people, trees, cafés, noise, music, shops and architecture you could find this cul de sac rather hellish. A northern town on a Sunday for a stranger can make a pretty good contender for the Hell stakes. I wrote about Liverpool on a Sunday years ago in not too dissimilar circumstances and the natives wrote back to say I had maligned their beautiful city. But there is an impression you get at first glimpse which is the freshest you'll ever have. From then on nerve endings that are in pain will gradually withdraw and tolerance will set in. That is why the brain shuts down when in pain and goes to sleep.

It is now time to warm up.

9.10 a.m. the following morning

The 09.00 from Darlington to Kings Cross on Inter-City. England flies past us in a moving conveyor belt of green, while up above fat grey/white suddy clouds loiter suspiciously. But on the left side of the train the sky is a brilliant, perfect, crystal blue – through the wide screen windows distant, misty azure hills. Then we pass small copses, woods in deep green, old brick barns nestling in the jowls of the hills surrounded by purple gorse. The train seems like a zip dividing the countryside into two parts as we skim through the centre. Now wide, new mown fields, green then yellow, almost paint-smooth, the familiar patchwork we see from a plane. Now a new-mown field in rich mud, ploughed up, ready and waiting to take seed. The clouds are growing thicker and heavier, hedgerows, windbreaks, now a pond with a mirror-like surface reflecting a flock of crows spotting the air like crotchets. Then out of the darkening sky, a shaft of sunlight set a cornfield ablaze in golden light, that strange and marvellous mix of dark skies and sunlight.

Last night the show was terrific except for a blip in *The Tell-Tale Heart* again when concentration weakened for a moment and then the demons leapt into the gaps left by the defences and fed on the coagulate gore of my fighting spirit, but I kicked them out again. How they taste and smell blood.

(We pass five, huge, belching chimneys in the distance, those wide funnel-shaped ones and they are forming a noxious halo above them that seems to hang in the air. Announcement: *'Customers should change at York.'* 'Customers?' Not passengers, or travellers, but as if we were shopping in Tesco's for fish. So not 'travellers' which is too poetic and neutral, but the nice northern, gritty 'customers'. Now we're at York and there are dozens of bikes the customers have left at the station, all clustered together like wasps around a honey pot. We rest and the train takes a breather at York, which is a dowdy yet clean station.)

★

Once you're inside the theatre you could be anywhere in the world since the comforting dark womb of the auditorium feels like a home, even though it also doubles as a hot-plate on which you dance. Actors love theatres that have a Victorian feel to them and yet they are also arenas of pain, nervous sacrifice, fear, torture and exhaustion. The late director Tyrone Guthrie also compared them to symbols of human sacrifice since the first theatre was the sacrificing of live offerings to appease the gods and we still call the upper circle 'the gods'. So here was my arena for the night, the altar on which I have to sacrifice my modest show for the entertainment of those who have come from far and wide to see me and I must cast aside all other worries or nags that line up at this special time. Your blood is tastiest before the sacrifice and the vampires, sharks and demons hang around with their dry rasping tongues. My dresser brings in my cuppa and on goes the slap. In twenty minutes I am someone else and no longer me. The potion is working and my cells are turning me into a killer of Poe's creation. The obsessional man. I started the piece and held my freeze for longer than usual as if I couldn't bear to leave the womb and go out into the world. I hid for a few seconds longer in my tableau freeze and then slowly, very slowly, unfolded.

One hour later I am in my dressing room, my make-up sliding down my face, washing it off and having a cuppa ... sheer relief. The first hour over. (The clouds are heavier, weightier as we leave York, dark and sinister, ready to drip their load. *'Customers for Skegness should change at Doncaster'*. I remember going to Butlins Holiday Camp at Skegness; it being memorable for being kicked out for writing a mildly lewd comment on a 'Lost and Found' form and sleeping the night on the beach-front bus station in Skegness.)

I change for *Actor* and it starts at full strength, bang full of energy and the laughs explode like little grenades going off all over the house and then I missed a whole chunk of the text. I have lost a page and must go back. As I am acting, my reserve brain is calculating the cost of going from the beginning and so I do, but emphasising it so as to make it look like the repetition is a deliberate part of the unemployed actor's routine. It works and I picked up the threads and did a quick linking join and was back on the rails. I was able to stitch it together and Mark Glentworth, my music man, keeps a sharp and sensitive eye on the proceedings, adapting the music as we go along. Finish. Leap to the corner and change for Dog...

Get into Doc Martens, Union Jack T-shirt, glance in the mirror and it's okay. March on to the very appropriate strains of the Sex Pistols' 'Anarchy in the UK'. One sleaze-bag, posing as a hackette journalist, having hacked her way through everything about me, even had the temerity to criticise my use of this opening music. In fact Johnny Rotten who came to see my show was well chuffed. She thought my character should have Rod Stewart! Mind you she hated everything about it but most of all hated life and everything in it except herself. But tonight the audience lapped it up and I started at full power. There was cheering at the end from a young, vibrant and positive crowd who had come from all over the district and as far as Newcastle. The theatre director tells me that it is unusual to see so many under-forties and I was glad if I was the magnet that was able to draw these black, brown, red and blonde heads out of their homes to see me. As little else was open Paul, Mark and I dived into an Indian restaurant opposite the theatre and had an excellent feast – a wonderful jalfreezi and finished with koftee. The Indian waiter asked for my autograph saying that they had some celebrities from the theatre here the previous week who were doing Agatha Christie.

I crawled gratefully into bed but was woken in the middle of the night with the scream of the fire alarm, which turned out to be false. However the *customers* in the hotel all traipsed down to reception, giggling and looking sheepish with men making jokes like. 'I thought it was a bit loud for my wake-up call' and the women kept saying, 'Oh, I couldn't 'arf do with a cuppa tea.'

★

Breakfast. One hour to train. I asked for grilled tomatoes on toast so I could get ready slowly. A voice said, 'Oh, a cooked breakfast in your room will cost you a £5 supplement!' 'Forget it!' I said and slowly crawled down to the breakfast room. It seems that nobody in this country can shift a leg, for which they are already being paid, unless they are sucking more money out of you. Before I could speak, I had a tea bag soaking in a pot and some lukewarm toasted white bread with the texture of recycled loo rolls. 'No, no croissants.'

Still, the room was pleasant and I could at least see Darlington High Street and humans. So I gratefully escaped the Hôtel du Morgue with its symbol of the swallow which would have certainly died miserably there. As the taxi sped past the grim façade of the Civic Theatre I was not unhappy that my sweat has now stained that stage. It was a good evening.

9
Samba in São Paulo

One Man went well last night except for a slight tear in my concentration and my 'hard-on' went for a few seconds. I sweated like a garden sprinkler and in the dressing room my make-up looked like one of those frescoes that you see in ancient Italian churches that have almost crumbled and are partly whitewashed over. Most of it had come off as if my character had melted. I recovered, sending masses of instructions to the brain for support and felt on an even keel again. To make up for my lapse I stormed into *Actor* and it was my best ever, so I regrouped my energies and *Dog* was so funny I even started to add visual subtitles.

After the show I went back to the small outside café and the cool evening air gently soothed my overheated brain. I drank a strong caiperena and then with Mark and Clara tried out the Avenida Samba Dance Club. I had been asking for some days now about samba and was determined, since we are in the land of samba, to partake of it.

We took a cab and the length of the journey was already ringing warning bells. He dropped us outside a building in the suburbs of Rio which looked suspiciously quiet. The newspaper kiosk in the entrance to the hall didn't bode well for the sweaty, salsa-pounding, hip-grinding, sexy, hot samba dance hall we were all looking for. However, we found the small box office and the guy let us have a peep inside, seeing that we were 'gringos'. We examined the huge hall with tables all around the edges. It had a raised area so people on the outer edges could see and yet was also wide enough for a mini dance floor off the floor. Everyone, at first glance looked suspiciously young but we thought what the hell, let's have a go for an hour.

We found a table on the raised area and we were served immediately with our caiperenas. Then the band came on and the rhythms of the hall started. I never saw such dancing in my life, as the band sent an electric current around the entire room and the spark brought inert flesh to life. Everybody moved, wiggled their feet, beat time with their hands, jogged their heads, moved their shoulders from side to side, snapped fingers and undulated their torsos, all while talking, drinking and eating.

The Brazilians danced – and what dancing! They knew how to samba and lambada and the men held their women who seemed to enjoy acting like rag dolls being hurled around. But this was an illusion since the men knew exactly how to handle their delicate yet strong animals. These volatile creatures in their arms allowed themselves to be twisted, spun, left hanging on their men's thigh like a beached mermaid, tossed into the air or thrown to the ground. In fact the women demanded this since it showed the men's dexterity in handling them. Sometimes they resembled the life-size puppets used by the Polish theatre director Tadeusz Kantor. The women melted and reorganised their bodies with ease as if they were cream being poured over the men, while the men danced as if they were preying, stalking, hypnotising the victim. Then the women acted like ensnared ones, succumbing, draping themselves around the men. They were like mating dancers, praying mantises, birds in heat spreading their wings. There were hops and twists and all this in the basic three-step rhythms of the samba or lambada.

No one looked inelegant but more beautiful the more they attempted, as if there was nothing they couldn't do with their combined bodies; no shape, form, twist or jive was not tried to extract some new sensation, some novel *frisson* of rhythm. The women were the sexual, dynamic ones since they appeared to be passive, to be taken, hunted, intensely desirable, allowing themselves to be carried on the waves of men's energy. The female must be even more skilled than the man since, fastened together, the man must guide and take charge but she must be certain of what he is doing and there is no room for sexual politics here. Here the samba is the politics. If the male is not dominant, doesn't lead, charge, possess and control, the woman will not know which way to go since her feet must interpret quickly or she will stumble. The male movements must have no uncertainty to them.

Her body is held firmly, the arm encircles her waist, she is made more feminine than ever. In this hall I see the full beauty and extreme lyricism of the female rhythm: the hips gyrate, the knees are slightly bent and the legs parted as the male leg must gently nudge and thrust and he may have to make intimate contact with her in order to lift or lower as the thigh thrusts forward and he arches his body back, and so the dance weaves and bounces. Here the male enables the woman to define and exemplify her form: the long line of her leg, her hair becomes wind whipping through long grass, her hips tightly packed into her dress as if she were painted into it... she becomes the woman of your dreams, unreal, fantasy, exotic, delicious and yet powerful. While he moves her, guides, commits arabesques, it is the female who inspires. I watch their faces as they are being led, thrown and twisted. They read the man's body as if perfectly at home, an expression of tranquil concentration.

10

The Pool of Light

Los Angeles – the last *One Man* show

The last night ended on a good note. I felt exalted, ecstatic and unabashed as I shot my hand into the air like I had won a race. I stood in the wings, having run off the stage and waited for the applause, a turbulent whirlpool of sound, to drag me back and to be sucked right into it. My ears were as the ears of cats, twitching to catch the response, like jugs catching the sweet drops of heavenly dew. The clapping continued and I was breathing hard in the darkened shadows of the wings hearing the applause as though it might be coins raining down on the pavement.

When in joy, hands are liable to come together spontaneously, as if you are unconsciously clasping the memory between your hands. And so the audience caught the night's memory between their palms, flattened it, absorbed it and like hungry wolves devoured it. Then my light smacked down on centre stage and I came to collect like a vulgar, greedy beggar licking up the smidgens of love in each clap, bowing my head to be stroked by the sound, craving their approval. I was drinking down the distilled essence of their gratitude for having been entertained for those two hours of their lives that they shared with you, and that can never be replaced. You have virtually corralled several hundred hours of human existence, woven it into a great cloth and tailored it into a made-to-measure performance. They would each go out wearing it in their minds until it slowly fades. For some it will not fit, while for others it will be as a glove.

So I leap into the golden pond of light and let their hands clasp and smack their sounds into my ears where they fly like birds and the approval is intense. The pain is over and so is the struggle to please, to serve, to sacrifice yourself as an offering on the altar where if the burnt flesh will be pleasing to Yahweh so may my sweating brow be pleasing to them. To remember the ritual of words, their special order, shape, sound, colour, inflection and pitch so that they may sneak past the defence of the audience and catch them unawares, in their vulnerable soft parts. Surprise their troops guarding the citadel of caution and suspicion. Be mad for those who cannot be mad. Act rebellious for those whose spirits would wish to be, but whose actions cannot, and allow them to journey with you. Soothe, seduce and even corrupt just a little as they take the germ of you out of the theatre until it slowly evaporates in the street. Then you march out on to the stage and collect your treasures that are poured sweetly in your ears. But also for you they are acting out a role, and they are not just 500 beating, anonymous hearts but a collective family, your approving ma and pa. You beg and cry for acceptance and approval from your 500 stepmothers and stepfathers.

You retreat back into the wings so that you may be called on again. It is a game to show you that they *still* want and love and admire you. So you play with them in the pretence of going off but allow yourself, almost reluctantly, to be dragged out and squeeze a few more drops out of the fruit, yes, lick up the last residue and then go home. You have performed for them and they have absorbed you and now they can all exhale in one brief response. You stand there and feel their exuding breath as warm as a large animal. You wait there and now they work, and even rise for you. Now as one group get up, they force the people behind to stand. It becomes a domino effect as nobody wishes to sit viewing someone's arse since they cannot clap that and must at least see the object of their efforts. So they rise even though they had no intention of rising, no intention in the world, but are led to this situation by the enthusiasm of the ones in front who want to demonstrate in a more physical way their adulation. Now, once again, you bow, strut and let the waves flow around you as the audience becomes one giant tap from which flows a stream and you surf on it and let yourself be carried by it.

Then you withdraw, only to dive into the river of their applause once again but God forbid the river should suddenly dry up. You are already on your way to the stage and the bodies of the audience, not anticipating your return, are now turning gradually towards the exit since it is a ritual in which you lower the lights each time so that they may fear never seeing you again. You are heading towards a dried-up river bed and are liable to crack your head open but they are ready to halt their journey for a moment more and almost as a reflex action extend you a few more claps, just enough for you to splash about a bit and not look stupid. You have, after all, withdrawn like a lover only to revisit with increasing ardour sweetened by the momentary absence. It is the pull and thrust, the ebb and flow of the tide. Your absence for a few seconds shows that you need them to respond, to show you that they want you back. 'So, please, oh please, maestro come back.' And then, moved almost unwillingly, you allow yourself to be pulled back by their swirling adoration.

Now the centre spot comes on again and is like the moon's reflection in a dark lake. I dive in and it is deep enough to bathe in its warmth. The uncertainty of your return to their midst, the sense that they may have not been prepared now makes them increase their volume. It accelerates, grows like a cascade of fruit descending on you from an overloaded tree that is shaken by a strong gust of wind and the ripe, sweet offerings are falling all around you. But risking it, I withdraw once again and the moon goes into eclipse. For a moment there is complete darkness, and just for a few seconds a visitor from space would find it difficult to interpret the meaning of a thousand hands clapping in a darkened space. While in the wings, hiding behind the cloth, a solitary man is standing, sweating like a criminal after some terrible act or an actor having left the stage waiting, like a drug addict, for his fix of applause. Everything is in limbo. The electrician has his hand on the button and we wait for him to create light and Lo and behold! the magic pool reappears as if summoned up by the energy of the audience. Once again I dive into it knowing it will be and must be the last time and so scoop it up and wallow in it, leaving slowly, greedily grabbing the last drips, scraping the vestiges of applause off the bone. Leaving gradually, first the body and then the arm like a lover parting as if for a long time. I have been sated and the holy oil of their blessing runs down my ears along with the sweat.

I go back to my small dressing room and then to the parking lot. You never clap a film and that is what I love about the live experience. You have all shared this one night together and it will last longer in their minds. Also, unlike film, your mortality will certainly ration the number of times you will be able to dive into that pool of light.

11

Bahamas

'You need a work visa.'
'Okay, I can apply for one.'
'No, you have to apply outside the United States!'
'I do?'
'Of course, that's the law if you want to work on this film.'
'So, where do I have to go?'
'Well, er... you could go to the Bahamas. You could go there...'

From the set of *Fair Game*, Miami, to the Meridian Hotel – in the Bahamas, charming old French villa, beneath a pink and pastel cocktail of clouds, and rum punch on the terrace. Peace at last. Attractive black people whose wrists are circled in chains of gold. Now the sky turns grey with blood dripping out at the edges and yet above the clouds is a soft powdery blue turning to aquamarine. But it's basically the same dead lounge seen in all the world's hotels, but will venture out on the town tonight to play Blackjack at the local casino. Suddenly recall the guy on the plane from Miami telling me he is sailing round the islands and how I admired his 'grown-up-ness' to charter a boat and know about such things as navigation which are no more familiar to me than flying to the moon.

The sky is turning deep blue now and the punch is getting to me. In the distance the clouds are reflecting deep red.

22 January

It's a beautiful, mild day but very windy and a touch cool... Last night went to the casino and won! I was losing $50 and so I got up and changed tables and then I won back my $50 and added a swift $70. What with all this excitement I was getting hungry and so I ate in the Oriental restaurant and ordered a chicken with broccoli which was so boiling hot it felt microwaved but I couldn't even begin to complain since the natives here are so genial and beautiful and utterly charming. What a change from all that Yankee dross. When I was leaving to go to the Bahamas to get my work visa I went to the production office to cash a cheque, and Andy Sipes'[1] assistant, seeing that I was there, takes the opportunity to ask me to try on another costume. For the sake of fun and to be bolshy in a jokey way I said, 'No way, I've already tried on umpteen costumes,' although of course I really had no intention of refusing such a simple request, merely wishing to act the 'temperamental star' for ten seconds. However, the assistant arsehole, devoid of the irony gene, responds tartly, 'I'll tell him that,' and off she runs to whinge and inform on me to her young runty boss and is so happy to be the bearer of evil news and show what a willing 'go-fetch' she is. I see her whispering to Andy thus fulfilling their prejudices about what a lot of nasty jerks we actors are and in a way relieved to have this confirmed since it is much easier for them to be cold and nasty than warm and loving. However, I walked over and showed a 'Hey, I was just kidding and don't get your smelly knickers in a twist' kind of look. But from then on

---

[1] Director of *Fair Game*.

the creature never spoke again. Then before I left, the head of stunts calls and asks if I know who normally does my stunts for me but my head was still steaming at the way the ugly bitch ran off with such eagerness to poison relations.

The Casino
Last night after my meal I sat down again and won continuously. The $10-wins were coming up fast and I doubled on 11 and so in a few minutes I got up after another $90. I have a system now to play for the duration of 'the shoe' and then stop, and so during the shoe you know you will only play for the five minutes or so and therefore you concentrate and play at speed until the last card and then get up from the table and leave. You lose when you keep staying since the tide will eventually turn and you must wait patiently for the dealer to shuffle the boring cards etc. No, just get up and stretch your legs, have a drink and then you later sit and concentrate like mad for another short intense burst. Like sprints. There should be at least three or four other players there but not a full table since it takes too long to get back to you!

It is going to be a beautiful day and it's good to get away from the film set since the dialogue is such rubbish[2] but I don't think about it too much since I continue to write a real screenplay – *Isle of Dogs* – sing *Carmen* under the tutelage of my private opera singer, explore Miami and learn *Coriolanus*.

23 January
Bus that scours the hotels and shaves off the tourists waiting outside picked me up. The driver is a young selfconscious, spoilt, good-looking man wearing a steel Submariner Rolex... the required accessory for serious divers. We arrived at what seemed a huge trading station or summer camp, a row of

---
2 I wrote this before the reviews trashed it!

huts overlooking a canal which bleeds into the sea. Several girls were processing the line and examining the forms we had filled out on the bus detailing our health and mental competence to dive and so on. I had to locate a flimsy wisp of a receipt the hotel had given me to show that I had prepaid since in the welter of instructions, paper, pamphlets, health forms, queues and demands, I had lost or mislaid it, whereby the surly tart behind the desk says, 'I don't know if you've paid. I mean, how will I get the *money*?!' I said, 'Please don't worry about the money since a quick phone call to the hotel will confirm it.' It had already been confirmed since the tour guide at the hotel desk gave names and details of the guests to the driver which happens only after you've paid the MONEY! However, I eventually found the little slip of paper and all was well.

After this I was shunted along to another station where a small mass of fat, thin, wobbly and somewhat obese men and women were nervously picking up their diving gear from a slim, cool, and fit Bahamian. His very presence seemed to be a perpetual comment on our opposite ways of life, between the healthy black and the Brueghel-like podge of the white tourists. He gave us a bag with instructions – don't put your weight belt in the bag – and after requesting the size of our shoes we hobbled on one leg like wounded gulls trying to fit one big bird-like fin because nobody thought it necessary to provide a bench. Maybe this was part of a deliberate humiliation process. Yes, my fin was fine and so I took my bag and shoulder bag – 'No you can't leave that here – ' to the next station where the tourists were trying on their wetsuits. Here there was a platform of sorts and I attempted to pull on what felt like a second layer of skin. After a while I managed to squeeze all the bulges into this blue sheath and zipped it up feeling like one of those suitcases you crush and kneel on. Now I was packed inside my new rubber skin and ready but then there was the hanging around routine like – where do we go?

In the meantime a couple of brightly plumed parrots entertained the tourists and one of them was doing what it likes to do, which is to nip you or crawl up your arm and so everybody who passed it said, 'Pretty Polly' and trundled to wherever they thought a crowd was assembling but as you moved towards the crowd they seemed vague about what to do next and shunted about making adjustments to their suits.

Three boats turned up that seemed ready to absorb the more serious divers or those who had their PADDI diving certificates. These divers went down deep and even double-tanked. They also looked slimmer and fitter than our casual lot, most of whom were just nibbled by the bug of curiosity to try out what looked so exotic in the hotel brochures and one or two like myself who had some previous experience in other exotic locations. It was something to do to pass the time as opposed to a real obsession with crawling around the ocean bed staring at sea-spiders close up.

Our group was still hanging around and we began to feel like victims of people with superior knowledge, the gurus who teach groups and are emboldened by being in charge of our bodies and minds to treat us with casual indifference. Where are we going, I wondered, and I asked a couple of old dears who were actually smoking but they didn't seem any wiser than I and so I went back to the hut where I'd registered and had all the business with the forms and actually hoped that the girl would be at least pleasant to me and not treat me like an imbecile inmate of a prison camp. 'Just wait outside...you're on the training course, right? You go to the pool.' We waited on a grassy verge until we were all ready...offering our novice shapes and sizes before experience weeded out the infirm, the nervous, the impatient; survival would be of the fittest. So we still waited and I got chatting to an Englishman who had been on the bus and was drawn like a clarion call to his simple grey-clouded English modesty. Now, in one of those strange quirks of fate, those seemingly improbable coincidences, as they say in the Ionesco play *The Bald-Headed Prima Donna*, where coincidences pile one on top of the other: 'What's your name?' 'Steven,' he says. 'Ah, what a coincidence.' I was tempted to see if we shared astrological signs and yes, almost, since his birthday was a couple of days short of my sign. He's Cancer to my Leo and unbelievably he lives a few hundred yards from me on the Isle of Dogs!

Then we all piled back on the bus taking us to the training pool. There was a disgusting package by my feet that looked like meat for a dog and blood was now seeping through the packet. We piled out again and traipsed over to the pool that looked like it belonged to a second-class hotel whose guests couldn't object too much to having their pool requisitioned a couple of times a day by shapeless rubber people. A couple of cut-price tourists watched with bleary eyes as these Martians flopped about in the water. The instructor was another young, smart, well-muscled American wearing his shiny, steel diver's watch and sporting some dive tattoos on his arm and leg. One was an octopus spread over his shoulder. We now got into the pool and practised 'equalising', which is to equalise the air in your body to the pressure outside by squeezing your nose. I often wondered why nobody bothered to mention this to me all those years ago when as a kid my ears suffered that terrible pain in my local swimming pool when I dived deep. After this we practised losing our snorkels and recovering them again calmly while holding our breath naturally. It's magic when you are without the breath of life and you put this nipple to your mouth again and feel it enter your lungs in great cool quaffs. Nothing else can make you realise how we should treasure the very air in which we breathe and how sweet it is.

One woman had already dropped out and she was a fifty-ish looking woman who chain-smoked at an unbelievable rate and now sat by the pool doing just that while we kept losing and finding our teat, equalised, and listened to our leader who treated us like the children we actually were in this art: *'Now don't go touching anything ... I won't tell you twice ... You touch anything and I'll inflate your belt and send you to the top!*' So we all resolved not only to abstain from touching anything but also hoped we wouldn't involuntarily be tempted to touch one of those extraordinary brain corals. However, the warning had whetted our appetites that we would actually be going somewhere out there in the mysterious sea since the concrete pool might have been our only experience of underwater breathing and the rest was a fantasy.

Now we tumbled back on to the bus once more and then on to the boat but before this the rubber strap on my mask broke and I was happy that it didn't happen down deep. 'Well, we can't check everything,' our leader laconically replied but I also noticed that he didn't even teach us the mandatory hand signals for running out of air and so on, or even the okay circle of first finger and thumb. Maybe he forgot. The boat trip was beautiful as we sped across the impeccable clear water, so crystal clear, transparent and full of promise and all hearts were uplifted as the boat sliced the waves. About a couple of miles out we anchored on some sandbanks, strapped our giant metal containers on our backs and performed this step into the water, which was really kicking one foot out into space, holding your goggles with one hand and your belt with the other. Suddenly I'm in another atmosphere and breathing away greedily and am reborn as a fish. We descend a rope but since there are so many of us I find myself waiting again, only this time on the bottom of the sea some twenty feet down. I see the boat's bow floating above me as if it was still somehow in the other dimension that we have broken through. Perhaps there is something atavistic about diving that sends minuscule blips of memory through ancient genetic codes. It seems so normal to be kneeling on the sea floor while the lumps of the world descend the line, fitfully, slowly and nervously.

I watched, as the blobs descended, each with its quivering sphincter and fear of the unknown since for most this was the first time. So slowly, like lumps of meat on a fisherman's line, they sank into the beautiful deep green gloom and I was craving to float down there, to imitate those childhood dreams where I flew over buildings with so little effort. Is this a tiny vibration reaching over the millennia of my fish life, when millions of years ago I existed in the sea and since our brains are comprised of billions of cells, perhaps in the very centre, they carry the earliest information of the past. Just as the salmon finds its way back hundreds of miles to its place of origin with no signposts using only its genetic map as a guide, so the cells of my fish life must still be there and there is a sense of profound calm and peace, a kind of tranquil equilibrium as if some deep microcosm smiles with the relief of 'returning'. So I waited to drift across the reefs but still beginners were fitfully descending, some halting halfway down with a problem and then I could see their fat arses returning to the surface while I was now getting cold and shivering down there making do with staring at some yellow-tailed fish that were now examining us with some curiosity. They had silver-grey fins and a yellow line across their fuselage.

AT LAST! We took off, following the leader like a long necklace of wriggly flesh. The corals we were forbidden to touch already looked rather worn out but still it was exciting to dive past electric blue fish so intensely coloured they seemed to glow as if the colour reached the zenith of its power. And so our circle swam around the boat for about twenty minutes and then I saw the grateful lumps slowly ascending to the surface after their little adventure with the deep. I was loathe to leave this peaceful Shangri-La, my oneiric underworld, and so I dawdled, letting everyone get on the boat and then I eventually broke water. As my face crashed through the liquid skin I felt I was entering yet another dimension so attuned was I now to the subaqueous life and the sun and wind gave me a pleasant surprise and as I gulped the air unaided I thought what an amazing thing air is that we can live off it. I had travelled a hundred million years.

Everybody back on the boat was now a changed person and there was a sense of exultancy at having had this primal experience, an almost out-of-body sensation. We shivered and giggled and shared experiences. I felt smugly like an old timer since I had done several dives over the years, in Mexico, Fiji, St Lucia and now the Bahamas. We still were shaking but warmed our bodies in the sun and stared with sparkling and fresh eyes at the blue horizon and felt as if we had been somewhat purged of our ontological weight and were spiritualised. Now we took pictures of each other, at least my new 'friend' Steve and I did as we unpeeled the second skin off our bodies, impersonating a banana. Of course and I swear this is unbelievably true, 'Steve', my namesake and neighbour had the *same* camera as me, which was a Canon ES, although his model was upgraded but only by the same distance as his home is from mine, and his birthday from my birthday. So we were able to understand each other and took some good pictures. 'Steve', my alter ego, was very happy and he had tried something he had never done before which is, after all, the point of a holiday.

12

A Place Called Homestead

Thursday, 16 February

A place called Homestead. Back on the set of *Fair Game*. The trucks race around the corner, slide, into a skid and I do good long-shot takes with my own dialogue. Worked well for a few takes even earning fulsome compliments from the stunt arranger but we did it so many times that when it came to close-up I mussed the words for a while but picked it up later. Our director, I feel has no warmth for actors or human beings in general and gives no encouragement and so you have to make your own judgement. I picked the scene up again but felt I had lost the zap I had in the beginning. Who cares, it's only shit in the end. The director wanted more 'something'... complains a lot, threw me out of sync when he asked me to try it too fast and I lost the style. Since I am a Russian who switches accents, I used a Texas one for this scene. Good. The dialogue is better but he doesn't encourage my inventions. He has a tin ear, so I have to beg to improve the 'dialogue' and lift it out of the rut when I should be encouraged. Money. What we do for it!

Everybody around the set wears heavy steel watches and the guys look swelled up like they're made of beefburgers, healthy, muscley, meaty, phoney. Denis, the first assistant, shouts for quiet with a huge voice like he was practising for opera. Cindy Crawford and I exchange a few thin words. My team in the film are the actors Jenette Goldstein, a funky red-haired actress who has her child in tow, and a Polish actor called Olek Krupa who will turn out to be a pal in every sense. A sensitive actor with a great deal of soul who puts up with the ludicrous *Batman* costumes and dribble of dialogue in the hope that we will all be able to create something from this abysmally vacant script which is a 'vehicle' for Cindy. Everyone is inspired to do their best at first but now deflation is setting in fast. Andy's direction to me... 'Steel balls!' Since he saw me clinging on to the strap as the trucks slid into position on the wetted street. The driver merely brakes with his other foot on the gas pedal and is impressive and something that can be learned.

Lunch
Then Cindy and Billy Baldwin do their scenes while we sit in the wagons and reflect on life. Had some lunch and spoke to Olek and Gustav, the other 'Russian', and had a few laughs. Nancy, Cindy's stunt double and girlfriend of the stunt arranger, comes over and talks about her bruises and the macho men she obviously is beginning to grow tired of. She sees herself more as an actress. 'I just thought I'd come over and chat to you guys!' as if to apologise and repeats it in various forms two or three times. There are several cops, who are security, feasting like panthers at the lunch table and some look well turned out, like they spend a lot of time in the gym. They look robustly fit in their well-cut, short-sleeve shirts, sporting shiny silver badges while on their hips hang their lethal weapons.

Joel Silver comes by and I quite like having the producer there watching. At this stage you feel like it is a father figure dropping by and you have this innate desire to please.[1] He

---
[1] Later I would see what an unpleasant and destructive father figure he would turn out to be.

wanted me to put those drops in your eyes which turn your irises a deep cool blue. 'Bruce Willis uses them!' But I had no intention of putting chemicals in my eyes for this pile of cobblers. Why is junk so difficult? The day is hot and I feel sweaty and everything around me is low and tacky and the director hardly directs us but barks out his demands while he sits with his snotty assistant. They creepily whisper together and smirk. This film is in grave danger. Feel overweight, stodgy and dull.

Friday, 17 February

The day starts at 6.45 a.m. with my pick-up. He's a regular guy wearing an ill-fitting wig. We both beef about the work as he drives me to the location outside Miami. He yacks on about O. J. Simpson, a subject about which every American has an opinion.[2] Meanwhile we are driving under a roseate dawn and the warm balmy air is soft as it streams through the open windows of the car and luxuriously cradles your face. He tells me it's gonna be a 'boodiful' day but adds for a little descriptive variety that there may just be a drizzle of rain later in the day. He uses the word 'boodiful' when discussing almost everything that meets with his approval since his descriptive powers seem content to let this word work for him in all contexts, saving him having to think too hard or get into a tangle. Whether it's the countryside, weather, food, people, the same epithet does for all. Now a little bashing for the film company that employs him and then the relative values of Stallone, Don Johnson and Schwarzenegger.

Arrive on the set which is a small town of trailers, trucks, costume wagons, food wagons, the small honey-wagons –

---

[2] If you knew where you were when Kennedy was assassinated you also knew where you were when the news of Simpson's damned acquittal came zinging through the airwaves. Carmen Du Sautoy heard it on her mobile radio while we were in Plymouth, I believe it was. We sat in the green room in a cosy part of England between the afternoon and evening show of *Salome*.

dressing rooms for the small part actors – and the obscenely large trailer homes for the stars, Cindy and Billy, and of course the smaller trailer for me. I'm a tad late so I shouldn't really go into the tent for breakfast where a sense of frostiness hangs in the air but I do. This is a frontier town and our grassy acre is a temporary city with all the facilities of food production, offices, clothing, electric power giving off heat and light and transport. It could be an army on the march.

The tent for breakfast is crowding up as the workers and actors arrive and enjoy what's probably their second breakfast since it's a freebie. The catering is first class and offers you, as usual out here, whatever you like. The main ingredients are already laid out on a long buffet table. I idly wander past the French toast, eggs, bacon, sausage, and throw two bagels into the toaster, scoop up some smoked salmon, tomatoes and cucumber and find a chair. My two colleagues are already tucking in, my Russian co-terrorists or whatever the hell we are supposed to be. The talk is animated, inspired in part by the early, fresh morning and the alfresco breakfast. There is also the camaraderie of being suddenly thrust into the maelstrom of human activity after the more rational private lifestyle one usually inhabits, seeing few people, spending much time either alone or with your partner and few friends. The intoxication of being thrown into a teeming mass of humanity causes actors either to withdraw to trailers or to suddenly find themselves thriving as group animals, excited, telling stories, confessing within a short time intimate details of their lives as if this was the real life and way to exist, in brotherhood and community. Also there's the sheer variety of people on hand each day to choose from and the possibility of bouncing from one to another. We have a huge hunger that we have for other human beings which is surrogately diverted by movies, books and TV but here they are now, in all colours, tastes, sizes, attitudes and it is a little like being back in school when we take such a torrent of human beings for granted. Yet in later life we somehow miss them and have to go to restaurants, since eating out at least allows you the privilege of dining with others.

A silver-haired assistant and trustee of the older school with mobile – or, rather, walkie-talkie – clipboard and other bijouterie of organisation hanging from his waist says it's time to get to make-up and so off I go but stop off at my trailer first to drop my bags. It's all as it was the night before as if I never left it. My costume is set out, black jacket and trousers and heavy knee high boots so I look as conspicuous as possible in my Russian bomber mode. I unload my shoulder bag whose contents will sustain me during the day when most time is spent in the trailer. A copy of *Coriolanus* to study since this a good time to work on it and get paid! A notebook to scribble in and a biography of Franz Kafka by Ronald Hayman which is quite extraordinary. I can almost smell the claustrophobic home Franz shared with his parents and sister. His almost compulsive writing turned from being his creative outlet to a prison in which he continually sentenced himself. Setting these on my counter in front of the mirror, I quickly flip the TV on. Only a news report of the OJ trial which we all know by now and the 'bloody glove' is now as familiar an icon of legal myth as the 'grassy knoll'.

I then step into the make-up trailer of mirrors and lights. I am sat down, bibbed, and my follically-challenged beard is trimmed amidst a thin stew of chatter. In the meantime I observe the make-up girls: one, demure, small and fashionably slim; the other with her hair gathered to one side like a wheat-sheaf sprouting out of her head, giving her a cutesy, loopy look like a dog with a floppy ear. She's friendly like someone working a small Joe's Diner in the middle of the sticks and is shortly to be sacked because she's too nice. Jenette Goldstein is being made up and is wearing a most ridiculous gymnastic costume throughout the film as if she was just going for a work-out. I learn Jenette was at my old drama school in London which was a real second-division place that you had to crawl out of in later years since the stigma rather sticks and you didn't say it exactly with pride. Now I hear it's much better.

My thin straggle of beard has been trimmed to its mandatory four-day growth and I decide to stroll to the set through the small day-old village of trucks and tents and into the real street in this backwater called Homestead. It's getting hot since it's going to be a 'boodiful' day. Jenette walks with me since she doesn't care to walk alone in that outfit with its short legs cut off at her thigh and so tight she has to keep pulling the leotard out of her arse where it keeps trying to sneak in. She has been training and of course looks super-fit.

I arrive at the video store where Cindy Crawford had taken a quick shelter and had used their computer facilities placed at the disposal of her and her rescuer cop, Billy Baldwin. I am the bad guy who is to extract information about the girl from the owner and of course this cannot be done without first inflicting the most massive amount of brutish, stupid and ridiculous force. This is to be enacted, take, after dreary take, by the new supermoron of the industry. There's little noise, around the store as the usual battalion of grips, gaffers, assistants, focus pullers, camera operators and 'associate producers' hang around, quietly going about their business until the lighting is ready for the next set-up, which is to be me. By the laws of motion, this small army is held back by the slowest element. There are guys here that are dressed as if for combat. One of the guys looks like a body builder, his huge muscular body neatly sculptured by a tight vest and made even more menacing by a shaved head gripped by ear-phones, ultra-light ones with a small mike in front so that he is in constant touch with the set. His job is to bring different lenses and cameras when it is required. On his belt hang the gizmos necessary for any emergency, even a terrorist invasion no doubt, plus (and most weirdly) a couple of animal pelts are also hanging there so he feels he has something of his own and is not just a human cupboard. He wears shorts as they all do and a heavy steel watch. A sour air of macho-ness which is always a pervasive pong on action films permeates the set like the air of a men's locker room except the smell is aftershave rather than armpits. But it is also a flammable quality apt to be set off by the slightest spark... too dry, lacking a little feminine moisture. The guys joust and yell instructions, beef around, gossip wickedly, send each other up and generally keep the atmosphere from getting stale. Few women are employed in any real capacity except to wander around fixing up make-up. As already noted, the director has a female assistant and she is almost always by his side like a colostomy bag, which in a way she is. She shares his every thought and wimpy sneer. From time to time we hear his distinctive laugh emerge from behind the TV monitors from where he organises the action. Why is making a film such a humorous business? Now he's suddenly absent on a recce some three miles away and the crew seem momentarily rudderless. We all drift around each other waiting like flies idly buzzing around a piece of old meat which this film is certainly on its way to becoming, clubbed to death with the blunt tools of the director's imagination.

The head stunt manager, a very robust and healthy man of Italian extraction says, 'You'll be needed for the first shot.' This is when the manager of the video store goes crashing over the counter as I hurl him across the room. The Cuban double is already being padded out and prepared and these moments are quite dramatic since the only real element of danger or excitement in the film is where the stunt man goes into action. Brave is the word. The double has had his head shaved to match the actor and a wig is perfectly designed to match the half-moon tuft at the base of the actor's skull. When I come to do this, the big stunt man, Charlie, shows me by demonstrating on me, grabbing my arm to show how I should swing him to send him flying. 'Show the effort in the teeth,' he advises and encourages me to copy his own grimace strained effort as the lips stretch and Lo and behold! there go the teeth looking all hard and determined. Mind you, as he held my arm I did feel his huge strength coursing through me like an electric current.

I'll handle this stunt, I thought. There's a lot of wandering around as you're called in to line up the shot since the cameraman needs something to focus on and to know where you might move and to measure that distance as well. The focus puller keeps checking the distance, as well he might, for to be out of focus is the greatest sin on Earth. Once the distance is established, a mark is put on the floor and you have to hit the mark. Now you're released for a while. The temporary stand-in now replaces you so that the lighting man can do his stuff. It's like a fish tank with everybody wandering around checking bits and pieces, circling, twisting, being attracted to one member of the human race for a moment and then another, exchanging some badinage, grabbing a coffee from Kraft services (which is basically a table of snacks set up during the day to fuel compulsive nibbling and is serviced by a catering firm who seem to do this for all the film crews) and then returning to the set, and always waiting.

So you sit down in the chair that has your name on it on the canvas back and read the simple news of the *Miami Herald* which has no arts column or reviews since little theatre or drama really exists except for the large touring shows. It's like a city without a brain. A theatre tends to link like-minded spirits and enables a community of such souls to form but here there is no way of finding this out. Only trash bars like Bar None, where models go and sit talking puke all night to like-minded idiots. In some theatres you can bathe in the knowledge that others exist with whom you have values in common. There is also safety in the knowledge that in the anonymous plains of Mammon there are people who are prepared to support the spirit and not just lazily slump in the modern movie house with its over-amplified sound, crap content and the stink of popcorn amidst the slurp of sucking straws. That unites the slump slurp slop society and one doesn't wish to be a part of that.

I turn the page of *USA Today* and see the same happy

gormless face staring out with that look to the side so that the eyes swivel naughtily to the reader. This unbelievably dreary woman dishes out the showbiz chatter which seems to concern less the art of the film than a dirty gossip's prurient interest in how much Stallone gets for his next movie. Her obsession, which she transfers to her dumb audience, reduces the reader to an ogling idiot jealously comparing their lot. The deadly virus has even affected England and at a recent deadly boring film awards, I had to hear of the millions of dollars taken by that puerile *Four Weddings and a Funeral*. I suppose if Shakespeare was around now his name or value would be determined by the box office. What did Wagner gross at his own opera house? In the end the ugly pursuit of grosses leads to the deformation of the art of film into porno violence. After finishing this garbage newspaper, I wandered into the area where the snacks are kept and absentmindedly poured myself a cup of coffee, squeezed some honey out of the honey pot, nibbled a biscuit and chewed some sliced peppers. Every so often a man comes around with frozen shakes which is a typically nice American touch. It's going to be a hot day.

We're back on the set, now that it's lit and the stunt man is thrown over the counter. The stunt director grasps the stuntman's belt in order to lift him more fully into the throw and suddenly the victim looks vulnerable since normally only children are held in this fashion. Denis, the big beefy blonde first assistant, lets out his operatic chords to shout for quiet and KERRRAASH! he goes and even the table collapses on impact.

The director sits behind the monitor and watches since they can no longer gauge the action from the floor but sit far away trying to approximate what it will look like on a small screen thus completely missing the danger, the excitement and the very real skills of the stuntman. Since it is only a slightly fuzzy image on a small monitor, it will never really satisfy and so he says, 'Let's do it again!' I thought the stunt was perfect and we should have moved on since the stuntman often goes at it with such a will to make sure that he doesn't have to repeat it, as with each repeat the odds on getting hurt significantly increase.

Two cameras recorded it but we went no less than *three more times*! Each crashing over the counter was accompanied by video sets shattering and equipment flying and each time I feared for the stuntman in the hands of this felon director. I have heard too often of injuries and deaths caused by thrill-seeking directors. It's over, but no... if that's not enough, the stuntman is kicked and shunted once more over the table like a human football being passed forwards and backwards.

Now gradually I enter the scene. First my feet are seen as the victim rolls to my feet. This is also shot two more times. The director reminds me of a Roman patrician watching Christians fighting with gladiators and licking his lips. I can take no more and my conscience drives me to confront the director, my juvenile master, to say enough is enough, surely! But these pleas for mercy only seem to whet his sadistic appetite as if I had drawn attention to his perverted tastes and thus he revelled in the role. He had of course no concern or compassion whatever but wanted to show how tough he was with a steel will to give the audience in the arena the greatest thrill possible. No matter what the costs. Meanwhile I am still waiting, and time is running out with all these dives over shop counters. The stuntman is a gladiator and is paid well for his crashes and the audience is the hungry beast. The plump tart sticks to the director's side like shit to a blanket with her dumb brutish adherence to all his whims and even more menacing, her inability to make a bridge between the actors and the director. They remind me of a couple of mean sneering school-kids with a constant coarse laugh that emanates from behind his monitors. Quite revolting.

The sun shines over Homestead and the heat is increasing. Three years ago a giant storm punched its fist right through the town which lies just at the beginning of the Keys – that stretch of ink spots that tails down to Key West. I'm called back on the set and because we are only actors dealing with dialogue we're expected to get on with it since we must get to the next piece of 'ACTSHHHHUN'. We're in a bit of a hurry now given that the stunts took so bloody long. However, I was trying to create something using my own dialogue and the director was patient enough to hear it and to know that it might have been an improvement on the script. So the video store manager once more rolls to the floor after being kicked by my accomplice who, curiously, appears to be wearing a swimsuit as if she just wandered in off the beach.

As a quick piece of research for the scene, I had picked up and leafed through one of those insanely technological magazines that were strewn about the video shop. It was mainly written in the jargon familiar only to those converted to its arcane religion. Of course children spend many happy and solitary hours playing these machines which inevitably corrode all sense of a world outside and the adult world uses them to communicate on cyber-net since it's easier to reveal only your thoughts and leave the discomforting reality of your body behind. So anyway, I picked up the magazine and conned a few words of technical jargon or 'technolese' which I mockingly used as the semi-conscious video store manager rolled to a halt at my feet, as if I had not just beaten him almost to death, but just dropped in for some equipment. I improvised some dialogue rather than use what was there which was some robotic text like 'Vere is de girl. Speak or I'll kill you!' -type of thing. It went roughly like this: 'Whilst I'm here, I'd like a desktop video with super-editing facility and colour management and throw in a few floppy disks!' Said of course with a degree of irony. Joel Silver watches on one of the many monitors stuck all over the place and the reaction from cast and crew seemed positive and elicited a few laughs in the rehearsal. We shot a max of three takes and I got it right all three times. I was relieved that my second real day of acting was over and that I was on the button for the text. Since in the shot I was looking down, they shot me from the manager's point of view and I stared down on to a little white tape that represented the man's face. It would have been a good shot and was in fact a good shot. In fact several days later the assistant producer made a point of telling me how great the takes were. At this stage I worked in good faith, firmly believing that I could create an interesting and mentally dangerous character for the film since the director and I had discussed it and he had encouraged me to 'improve' the dialogue. So I was pleased with the morning's work, naïvely believing I would continue to work, in this vein and make something of it.

I broke for lunch with a sense that I had made a head start into the guts of the movie and although it would be a long climb I felt I had established a foothold. The director was in a hurry to get moving, having spent all morning with his beloved human football and we had exchanged a few sparks but nothing to catch fire. Let me create them, that's all. A Russian extra who had been watching in the monitor passed me a few fulsome compliments which trickled warmly into my ear and helped to melt down the hard accretions of neglect. The director says nothing or throws a shaving, implying that it was okay. The Russian is meant to be one of the bodyguards for my character. He was tall, handsome and powerfully built and another one of those ubiquitous 'trainers' in Miami. The tent was waiting with a long buffet table groaning under the weight of the goodies. Just grab a nibble of salad, pass on the steaks, T-bone or otherwise, fish, veg, lobster.

For a blissful moment I *am* happy. My chore is over and I overcame the sweaty, nervous anticipation that tries to wind its tendrils round my throat and tense me up. I had however the second half of the scene after lunch. My temporary euphoria put me in a more sociable mood and so I breezed around our small city state and observing a group of smiling and welcoming faces decided to join the extras table. After the sour tension of the professional element I found them to be charming and pleasant and enjoyed the attention of young and pretty people who did not conceal their delight at having one of the 'stars' sit with them. Then in the same convivial mood I chatted to our marvellous caterer, a plump, jovial Italian-American and posed for a picture with him. The big healthy Falstaff popped out of his catering truck where we usually saw him like Mr Punch and solemnly placed his big arm around my shoulders the way you are supposed to for pictures, which for some reason nearly everybody does, but since he didn't want to offend me with his attention he placed it on my shoulder so lightly that it felt like a bird had landed there. So then the sky, the heat, the low puffy clouds, the quiet of Homestead, the street with the video store, the coffee, the fruit slushes, the executive producer sitting perpetually on his chair, welded to the mobile phone, the wandering up and down, squeezing the honey-pot for the coffee, chewing up the last few shreds in the awful *USA Today* like a bone that hasn't quite been licked clean, sucking some extra flavour from the screenplay which I rewrote anyway, all fitted together in a nice mosaic.

I am eventually called on the set to shoot the remainder of my scene. My comrade in the scene is my new found ally, Olek, who has merely to hold the victim, the store manager's assistant, by the hair and throat. Olek is already deeply frustrated as a human being and actor and needs to do more than stand around looking 'wicked' Anyway, I point my gun and discharge my newly written text. It sounds okay and I felt it gave something quixotic and poetic to the character so that he wasn't just an automaton. We do a take and I am told, in a brilliant piece of directing, that I am 'pulling faces'. I lower the temperature but it feels less sharp. The producer, Joel Silver, is always strolling around his property like a basking shark dressed in a natty two-piece outfit of matching shirt and pants and seems to possess a lot of these. The pants are soft like pyjamas and the full shirt drapes over his guts somewhat. He sniffs at the monitor to see if what he is being served is up to standard. He is also perpetually on his mobile phone which may go towards explaining the crazy outbursts he is famous for since recent scientific discoveries have produced reliable evidence that the microwave used for the mobile, although infinitely smaller than the one used to cook your chicken, can, with perpetual use, fry a tiny part of your brain! He exudes the air of one who is used to power. He has an attractive blonde assistant with him in tow and she is one of the many assistants who like tiny fish feed off and clean the larger fish in tropical waters. They're actually called goper fish while here they are the gofers. Joel is at the moment walking up and down as he talks to the world through his dog and bone. His head is slightly back as if taking in the scenery and he is raving away.

My work is over fast and in three takes. As a compromise, some of the ordinary dialogue from the script is retained although the clichés get somewhat stuck in my throat. We don't row and I seem to have established a work pattern in which I rewrite and invent and pass it to Andy for approval. He makes one or two amendments and we shoot. I'm already down the road and away. My grey sweater with its roll-neck which irks me is peeled off, thrown on the couch like I had sloughed off a bad skin and gratefully I put distance between myself and the set which is already history. Billy Baldwin gets out of his limo as I am leaving. 'There are rumours they're going to use me,' he says wryly, already becoming too familiar with this director's methodology. There is a collective sigh of relief when the day is eventually over and everything is allowed to collapse back to the routine of real life. I am dropped off at the Biltmore Hotel, one of the most beautiful in Miami if not the Earth. The air is warm. Trouble is, what to do with all this freedom.

P.S. All my improvisations were eventually cut, however, the film sank without trace.

13
A Miami Health Club

Everybody here seems to have a trainer, someone to cajole and pamper them. The gym at the Biltmore Hotel is a meat market where the predatory trainers eye up the potential in the slack bodies of the rich. Self-indulgence reveals itself in the wealthy with tell-tale signs of pouchiness and flabbiness and these are the clues the hard-bodied, non-rich sharks hone into. Usually they pander to their puffing clients but if they have an hour or so between two flabs they are liable to roam around the gym, chat you up and volunteer their services to demonstrate the complicated machinery, and even spend some moments giving you a free sample, explaining the mysteries of the Nautilus machines with their counterweight system.

These inventions resemble some bizarre contraption of torture, a device of machiavellian complexity, and you become part of this thing that you manipulate by pushing things together, or pulling them apart or hauling things down or heaving parts up with your shoulders from beneath or you may even dip yourself between. You might, while you are dragging yourself up, enjoy the illusion of lifting your body in what we used to call 'pull-ups', but now the machine subsidises your lack of strength to lift your weight, and allows your flaccid biceps to lift just what it can and you can happily indulge yourself by merely imitating a pull-up and no one will know just how much you are being loaned, unless they check the digital read-out. You may rest your arms on a cushioned surface and do a bar curl by curling the weight over your elbow and letting it slowly down again whilst ogling those expanding biceps. There will be a weight to push, pull, heave or shove for nearly all the muscles of your body, and if there is some little area of your anatomy that you wish to isolate and give attention to, your trainer will be glad to focus on that little patch and bring it into line with the rest of your emerging crop of muscles that hopefully will sprout after all this tending. Your body becomes your clay to shape and mould, to tease, and to strain the sweat through.

Music sends its slush through the gym inducing a kind of dozy euphoria of nowhereland where all is well and the-world-is-*here* kind of feeling. While pop music plays, life's okay. Let's try warming up first to get those muscles nice and elastic and you head for the treadmill which resembles a run for those who can't be bothered to go outside in the fresh air but would rather do it in the tepid vaults of the gym. It doesn't quite feel like a run since the treadmill recedes behind you and so you merely have to lift your legs but the sweat obligingly oozes out to your satisfaction and you exchange the trees and smells of grass after rain for the image of your sweating face bobbing up and down in the mirror facing you. This gives you something to look at while you count the seconds, continually checking how many laps you have achieved and how many goddamned minutes you have left. You increase your speed for a final little daring spurt which leaves you puffed and scrabbling at the controls to decrease it before the thing hurls you off like a piece of unwanted garbage.

After a while one needs to pass a glance at one's neighbour, comparing your performance to their own bobbing body bouncing up and down as they too stare at themselves with rapt attention. Nothing shall escape their fascinated eye – not one drop of sweat nor bulging vein throbbing in the neck, nor pained expression, shall not be of the most compelling and fascinating interest. The onanistic element is strong here since this is an exercise you cannot share with others as you did in the old days of the sweaty smelly gym when you worked with what they call free weights and two greasy blokes with grubby shorts lifted the barbell over your head.

Then you would lay on your back watching that pole with two big steel ears slowly descend on to your stretched arms. You take a hand's-width measure from the end of the bar to determine which part you will grip to give you the maximum brace and cry out, 'Okay!' and then they let the weight pour into your hands and run down the length of your arm. You let the weight descend to your chest – most often protected by a towel – and then heave and push it back again with straightened arms. After a few 'presses' your arms tire and so your back starts to arch to add some leverage in pushing the thing up, followed by the pelvis rising in support of the spinal arch. Meanwhile your colleagues are shouting encouragement: 'Go on... bit more... nearly there.' Your face has turned puce and your teeth are set like you were about to commit murder, and the voices around you are rising as if their words were forming small balloons of encouragement under the weights. Sometimes they'll even put a couple of fingers under the bar to ease your agony by that couple of pounds per side which is the difference between success and failure. You '*uuuuggggh*' your way till the arms are satisfyingly locked and with a nod of your head they snatch away the burden from you and at that moment you are deliciously liberated from the steel bar with its great saucers which then is set upon the metal cradle awaiting the next man.

Now the next man is on the bench shuffling his arse down it until he feels he is in the right position to receive the weight and is adjusting the towel on his chest, taking deep, sniffy, preparatory inhalations as if he was sucking energy out of the air. He is a serious dude and has found some chalk to rub on his hands so that the bar will grip and you move to his side ready like a willing slave to obey his demands, which might be a request to add another twenty pounds on each end. You swiftly unscrew the bolt that prevents the weight from sliding off, pull it off, pick up a ten-pound weight, all that mirrored by your colleague on the opposite side, slide the nut back, tighten it and slowly lift it and then lower it on to your comrade's chest. Now again the ritual of groans is enacted interlaced with encouraging murmurs from the watchers. This was the past.

PRESENT: On the treadmill three figures can be seen running as if forever without getting anywhere and for a moment look like a trio of horses running neck and neck that will never reach their goal. They stare into their thoughts. In terms of the aesthetics, the new-age gym produces the most horrible sights whereas the old BO-and-dirty-T-shirt gym was always visually dramatic: arms bulging, veins writhing, sweat popping out, guys skipping, gritting their teeth, bodies hanging from wall bars which then concertina up to crunch those abs, and of course the bonding. One man will hold your ankles while you perform your ab crunches and then you do the same for him and so it goes on. Here it looks like Hell. Isolation. You can spend an hour and neither speak nor have any contact with anyone. The world of the rich. Loneliness and separation.

The most horrible exercise to watch is the step machine that more than anything resembles Brueghel's *Journey into Hell* or *The Torture of Sisyphus*, with the endless climbing and getting nowhere since the step sinks down as soon as you mount it while at the same time the other leg goes up and so the routine is repeated and this produces a stupid-looking wriggle of the arse from side to side. The hands are held slightly splayed apart while the arse seems to be separated from the rest of the body so while the protuberant bum is doing all the work the face takes on a dazed empty expression, vacant, going nowhere, sitting-on-the-loo kind of look. At least on the treadmill you have to run, keep your balance, check the dials and so a tiny bit of brain is required but this is pure lobotomy. A tight butt is the goal and so the face as it sits atop the treading feet seems to have removed itself from conscious and responsible thought, drained of purpose, motivation and sensitivity. The face turns from time to time to the source of a sound like a chicken being disturbed while eating its grit. This is a machine which for biological reasons seems to be much favoured by women, and on a good day you might have the fortune to see a row of twitching arses resembling battery hens. Some will read a magazine while treading their lives away and the worse the torture or mindless the exercise the greedier the face: mean and greedy for a harder body and tighter billiard ball for each cheek. Swimming in the sea of sweaty narcissistic endeavour, the sharp-eyed sharks are slowly sussing the scene; the trainers, muscled like armoured trucks, are attending to their middle-aged, anxious clients, interpreting the laws of the machine world, this forest of steel technology. The clients hope that by merging themselves into the maw of the metal monster for a few hours a week, a corrugated field of muscle will be revealed under the snowy, indolent fat.

A woman coated in make-up that ensures that she cannot sweat from a face that has been severely clipped by the knife sits on a bike machine pedalling while she reads a fashion magazine. This keeps her contented while the image she cannot help but create as she casually cycles is one of sloth, vanity, greed and stupidity. You try to avert your eyes but at the same time morbid curiosity draws you back to the scene of horror.

14

The Explosion!

Tuesday, 11 April, 9.30 a.m.

Denny's Diner. Miracle Mile. Miami
At last found the café of my desires – Denny's. Open from 5 a.m. and big booth seats that enclose you while you sit and read the paper or write. Nice and private. A day on the film set of *Fair Game*.

The day started as it usually does with my being picked up outside the elegant Biltmore Hotel, Coral Gables, in a workers' van by a black lady who just sits there whilst I fumble with the door handle and eventually tumble in. I feel as if I am being picked up for grapepicking-like cheap labour. This is the van for all my gang of small part players and I resent it, since in the first weeks of shooting I was collected by a smart limo, the door would be opened and I was snugly ensconced having some pleasant chat. Now I feel demoted but for what reason I cannot devise. My driver is pleasant enough but doesn't talk much and I notice that she has fancy false fingernails with designs and tiny stones set in them.

The Explosion!

It was a 6 a.m. call for what was to be the last day and that was to reshoot the grande finale since it hadn't worked out on the last rendering when, surrounded by a wall of fire, I faced my demise. Producer Joel Silver didn't like it. It was dark when I stumbled out of bed, clambered into yesterday's knickers and sullenly crawled into the uncomfortable van where you sit high up on hard, heavy-duty seats instead of sinking into a slush of leather in the limo. I am third lead in this movie and I'm shunted around like a plumber.

Eventually we arrive and the dawn scorches a path across the horizon which is quite beautiful, so much so in fact that in my enthusiasm I have to point it out to the driver who turns obligingly to look and passes no comment. 'Drop me at the catering tent,' I request, since Joe the caterer will comfort me with a coffee and bagel before I crawl into another day on the set which is as predictable and sour as acid rain. The van stops but the only people I see sitting there are a quartet of people for whom I represent their most bitter nemesis, and isn't it curious that they are huddled broodily together like a witches' stew?

I hesitate to clamber out of the van since even the merest greetings are anathema and we meet only on the set where the inevitability of work allows us to communicate purely on the deed in hand. Where there is free will it is nigh on impossible to conceal our mutual antipathies. We avoid each other, never sharing a lunch table, a coffee or any social grace, which is not difficult, given the large work force. But now just this quartet sit there, seething with their mutual and shared aversion to me. And for what reason? Only that I have a tendency to dislike allowing myself to be shat on for, God forbid, having an opinion. Of course, the fault is not altogether theirs since I am employed in an action picture to play a bad guy and this is not the kind of project that is meant to engage your cerebral activities but is meant rather to satisfy on a gut level, so it doesn't really behove me to try to turn a hamburger into *haute cuisine*. Therein lies the problem.

When faced with language, or 'dialogue', as they prefer to call it, with the variety of a traffic light, an automatic reflex action to survive takes over as one tries to imbue it with a degree of wit or human reality. You're desperately trying to save the soul of the character you are giving birth to on screen as if it is part of you. Like a dying man, your wish to live becomes intense and you find yourself begging the director to insert a line that may breathe some oxygen into the creature so that it can climb out of the swamp of clichés and join the world of human beings. Alas, the director loathes my attempts to rescue the formula bad guy and so I must suffer like the poor pigs who eat the swill of the various writers. Anyway he is too busy with the explosions which take up a great deal of screen time and whose 'rushes' are greeted with awe.

One of the cameramen sits there with him who makes a point of giving me directions that either are not clear or deliberately vague, so as to ensure some opportunity to deliver a barb when you get it wrong. He sits astride his camera wearing his shorts, cute pony tail and endlessly chews gum that shows his well-kept teeth. Perhaps his attitude is a reflection of his master whom he supports since they are always breaking out into loud cackles as they probably dip their victims into their verbal snake-pit. Next to the director is his plump assistant who is always smiling at something as if in her seventh heaven to be near the heat of power. We have not spoken in two months.

I wonder if it is easier to cause offence in America than in the UK since affluent societies seem to have a lower threshold of tolerance and react severely to anything not immediately available, like children whose wishes are always gratified. In the UK we are used to less and have our famous sense of humour to oil the cogs.

Joining and completing the quartet is the leading make-up artist whose tolerance threshold was so low and her self-importance so astonishingly high that she exiled me from the star make-up trailer, where I would try to exchange *bon mots* with Billy or Cindy, to the small parts make-up trailer, for no greater offence than coming in after a gruelling day with a cigarette which I hadn't put out. 'You can't do that in here,' she hissed, as if I were committing some form of self-abuse in public. She glared at me with arch self-importance and was not remotely able to inject some form of civility in her tone. I have a particular detestation for underlings who use rules to help them to spit on those whose shoelaces they are not fit to tie. These are the star-fuckers who live and breathe the hallowed farts of their masters. It did occur to me that in this hideous PC society, if a male make-up artist had banned an 'actress' from his trailer she would be quite correct in having the offending chap removed from the set, accusing him of every sexist male crime under the sun. Oh, how I love petty officials. However, since the bile was now beginning to affect me, the following morning I did manage to quietly inform her that while the film could certainly not continue without me, it could without her, plus a few other comments made with icy restraint. She muttered something puerile in return since morons aren't distinguished for their wit or they couldn't perform moronic acts. I went back into my trailer feeling as if I had vomited up a giant slug and of course much lighter in consequence. Justice is a purgative instrument of the righteous.

So as the van stopped outside the catering tent, I saw this gloomy little stew sitting together as if like a mould. I was wondering how many more people would join the mob and would I soon run out of allies or even neutral beings, since in any organisation, there will be personalities at opposite ends of the spectrum. What we laughingly call civilised is the ability to make allowances for our differences in order to create the object of our endeavours. Not much allowance here. However, I thought that by now the work force had polarised into 'for' and 'against' and I knew who my allies were and who the enemy was and HQ was sitting having their morning coffee while I groaned and wondered how to get out of the van. All of a sudden the situation was saved when Mark, the assistant director, came belting up to me requesting me to get changed quickly as I was in the first shot. He would bring the breakfast to the trailer. Phew! Relief. Mark was also an ally.

I stepped into my sanctuary, my trailer, stared at the paper cups with their slew of turgid coffee left there from the night before and climbed into my awful costume. Gunner, my make-up man and also my ally, has had to schlep his equipment from the silver trailer, from whence I am exiled, to the older one, but to tell the truth I prefer it in here anyway. We exchange the morning stories and circulate the general feelings of discord that circulates round this project, although that by no means suggests that the film won't be an enormous hit.[1] The stress of making this one may be the very factors that might even lead to it being a smash and the 'dailies' are greeted with an excitement unusual within the cautious eye of the industry.

I'm on the set. I wait for Cindy Crawford who arrives looking stunningly torn and ragged after her encounters with the 'bad' Russians of whom I am boss, and readies herself to be tied up. We had completed our 'scene' yesterday and this was to be the finale when she and Billy Baldwin make their daring escape. Cindy is everybody's friend and appears completely unspoiled by her fame and for a neophyte actress has an extraordinarily astute eye for detecting anything false. Billy enters, looking his sleek, trim, trained self, his affability hiding what I perceive is a sensitive soul and brings over a cup of cappuccino to Cindy since these are the perks for the stars only. I am standing there as usual being ignored since there is something that rubs off the bad guy and into real life almost unconsciously, just as the heroes are also endowed with superhuman graces and indulged. I'm used to that but Cindy's

---
[1] But it sank like a stone.

all-seeing eye notes that I am without the magic froth and offers me a sip of coffee. How sweet, given the almost paranoic fear on these shores of passing the dreaded 'germ'!

This morning I was being kicked by Cindy until I felt that certain sites on my body were beginning to rebel by changing colour and yet there was a stuntman employed ready to receive the blows and hanging around idly, his unmarked muscular body just hungry for the stout thrust of her heavy boot to his chest. I requested, after gamely receiving a requisite amount of blows, that the stuntman now took over. 'But you're in the shot!' bellowed our operatically endowed first assistant. 'But I also get the pain,' I retorted and I knew that given the sheer number of takes we do, the odds on my sustaining a fracture were shortening. Eventually the stuntman went to work and Charlie the stunt arranger says to Cindy, who is concerned about hurting anyone, 'You can kick shit out of him,' which she proceeds to do to the padded stuntman who enjoys each moment and I can mercifully sit out until the next bit of torture. Excuse me, the next shot.

In the end the director is your creator, your God, your Dr Frankenstein, to whom you entrust your soul and body parts, who will cut you to fit the image he has of you or butcher you. But it is his will how large or small you are, how ugly or charming, how visible even, since you may be just a voice in the distance while the camera lingers on the non-speaking reaction of the other actor. So you must have trust and not even begin to suspect that out of some vengeance, the special way you did that line or that gesture will never be seen and you will be framed to fit the bed that you must lie in. Framed – interesting double meaning.

I've always felt that the director must never be the enemy of the actors since we are in league together and the actor must feel that his contributions are not only worthwhile but necessary. He lives only to perform his or her role and is alone in a hotel, sometimes waiting for weeks to do a spit and a cough, or sitting in a trailer for hours on end just to be a face in the back of a van and so, please care for your actors for they are isolated, vulnerable people only wanting to give creatively of themselves. But if you become the dominant father, the restrictive teacher, the bullying boss who allows no flights of fancy from the child, then you will get sullen, miserable and dull actors who only dream of the end and count the days. An actor taps his childhood for inspiration and if it is continually denied it is like a child told always to shut up. Be quiet. No, thanks. No, no and no!! And so it is of all actors who work with imperious directors.

We are not allowed 'fun'. Sometimes we would sit in the Russians' 'wagon' driving round and round and round and hear hoots of laughter from the master and his acolytes while we all sat like bullied children, crushed and silent and waiting to 'Go again' and again. The cawing laughter was a private joke made public only by its rude birth of sound which tells us they are having a brilliant time, even if the laughter sounds like *schadenfreude*. You sit silently munching your own thoughts and we only hear the words. 'Reset' and we must do it again and again and again and we must dutifully do it and not question why, as might be usual. We just do it and even the first assistant becomes an accomplice only in looks. Then back to the trailer for a new set-up. Oh, bliss.

I'm in my trailer where I either freeze or boil but this has been my little country cottage for the last two months where I can read, write, fall into a fitful sleep or watch the ghastly telly. Since reception is so poor out here, I am only able to tune into Channel 49 which is the weirdest religious programme I have ever seen. A bunch of guys with bouffant Fifties hairdos, looking like waxen Tom Jones effigies, sing about 'Jeezuz' and how he loves you. They could be sleazy car salesmen or pimps with their thick gold watches and nugget rings. Then one tells a story of having lost a dear one and a thick gluey substance forms in his eyes as he tries to hold back the tears. Of course they are begging for money and it shocks me to think that such filthy trash is allowed to abuse the vulnerabilities of the simple, uneducated and naïve who are a growing and easily exploitable mass here.

Mark, my friendly 'caller', knocks and announces that we're fifteen minutes away and I am temporarily warmed by his cheerful affection and then Deborah in wardrobe makes sure I have a change of everything and her goodwill to me never varies. I make my way, stopping for a coffee and some good words from Joe the caterer, and it's as if I was warming myself up on the heat generated by allies before facing the big chill on the set. Gunner touches up the artwork, adding his few words and it seems like the set divides itself around you and you bring out either the worst or the best. I naturally choose to believe that I bring out the worst in those inclined to a more inflexible nature (euphemism for arseholes), those guarded by certain parameters that define their life style and are unwilling to step out but request that you should always step in. Here they're called people with 'attitude', which could mean those holier-than-thou types who are to be avoided at all costs and there are plenty out here. Fortunately my 'Russian' colleagues, who actually hail from Poland and South America, remind me of what real human beings are. So there are others from whom you bring out the best!

The day drags on and the director has devised a nice death scene for me where I am shot, blood spurting out of little sachets, set off by mini-explosives, and I stagger to save my gigantic fortune by reaching the computer which somehow is the key to the treasure. The ship I am on is on fire and the flames rage around me and like some insane devil accountant working in the administration of Hell, I try to steal the money that I can never spend. As I roast in the hellish pits, my rich gore is spewing out of my mouth and dripping on to the computer until I sink into oblivion, clawing at the keys like the *Phantom of the Opera*. Ah, the end! Or so I think. Billy, meanwhile, escapes with Cindy into eternal bliss while the devilish, machiavellian foreigner dies in his own machinations. Wholesomeness wins. Now Joel Silver is built like a wrestler and perpetually on the move. He possesses seemingly enormous energy, inspiring a mixture of fear, admiration and other emotions. He strides on to the set. He is not satisfied and wants more explosive backgrounds, a raging inferno and so we must do it again!

The next day. I turn up and my bags have been packed at the hotel ready for me to take off after one extra shot. Not relying on their finishing with me today lest I am put into a clock-watching tension, I am prepared to stay and chip one more day off my diminishing rehearsals for *Coriolanus*. The usual van picks me up, thus destroying my illusion that on the last day they might have been inclined to indulge me. I have to do the scene again and it feels like *déjà vu*, however, I will do it this time against a background of orgasmic explosion. 'Don't worry,' says the considerate associate producer, Tom, 'You will get the 7.20 p.m. flight.' But as I climb into my knee-length boots with buckles and black leather coat studded with more steely buckles, I am told that there is no camera available for the assistant to shoot a second unit retake. All three cameras are suddenly on the other set with Cindy and Billy and one begins to entertain dark ideas that your well-being is not at the forefront of their plans.

You even analyse the motives and will of the director and imagine that it is a game, and not merely indifference to your needs. This galls me since the existing death scene had been so good. Marty, the assistant, shrugs as if to convey heaps of meaning that he dare not give words to. No camera and so I again sit for hours in the trailer and write in my journal, trying not to believe that I could be kept simply because they know I have something to go to that means something to me! No, that's just my little paranoia let loose. I think of the witches' stew. In any event, I tend to think that the material maketh the

The Explosion!

man and what I am feeling is maybe a touch of culture poisoning. But I insist that they will not rile me and I shall keep my bosom clean.

The day crawls by and from my trailer prison where I keep the door open, I see people come and go, the make-up staff wandering backwards and forwards. The drivers sit idly all day doing nothing or playing chess on the front seat. Joe the caterer is preparing lunch and furiously chopping each time I go to the coffee nipple and get a refill. The sky is that washy Florida blue with a few white suds crawling across it and birds of prey wheel high in the wide open air and I sit and wait trying to learn *Coriolanus*. After all, Joel Silver is paying for this picture and should get a little of what he wants.

I have a large photo of Cindy and I together which I am a little reluctant to ask her to sign, but what the hell and ask Mark to take it to her with a request that she write something on it for me. It comes back an hour later with a 'It's been a pleasure' on it and I stow it away. Ah, Mark comes in and says that we are now going to the code room. Mr Silver is on the premises and that always means things will speed up. It's not really Andy's fault that he has to reshoot and that I have other commitments but since we all get caught up with how we value ourselves, we feel cheated and abused if we are bid less than our estimated self-worth. So we have to reduce the price somewhat in order to feel okay about it. But there has to be a limit, surely! So once more I haul myself on the set for another bout of blood-spitting, spurting, spouting, gasping, being shot, burnt, drowned etc. It's going to be hot.

I have always avowed that naturalism is bad for your health and the number of accidents and injuries always suffered by actors (of course, never the director) in stage fights with stupid weapons, is legendary. In film, of course, it is worse and one hears constantly of mutilation by fire, helicopter, auto etc. and stuntmen are the frequent victims who stoically accept utterly ridiculous demands since American stuntmen are the bravest I have ever seen. Already on this film two people have been rushed to hospital, one from fire and another from whiplash in a car crash and while such things seem inevitable on an 'action' film, they are not for me who has an ideological resistance to putting any kind of artist in a hazardous situation.

I arrive on the set for the death scene and explosions. A kindly fire expert advises that I could grease up the side of my face nearest the blaze. What!! Is it to be *that* hot that already anti-burn precautions are necessary? I'm not a fireman, I'm an actor whose face, hands and body are my most precious instruments. I am beginning to seethe at what I perceive is a gradual disintegration of any rights I have relinquished for the sake of the great maw of movie that sucks down everything like a big, black, amoral hole. Charlie the stuntman says, 'Look, it's easy, it just gets a little hot, that's all.' But the grease! I eventually try to reorganise my personality and imagine what a Connery or a Caine would do. Split. I refuse to do it on the grounds that it is dangerous and I have already seen fire accidents on this set. Charlie reassures and suggests a test and kneels where I will be clawing at the computer as I die in the inferno.

For the test they set off only one blast and although I am actually being shielded by Charlie, the noise sends me reeling. The fireman says it will actually be 50 per cent bigger! The whole crew are watching and waiting and Joel Silver comes on to the set. He strides on like a Sumo wrestler getting ready for a bout. 'I've done millions of these things. You seen my movies!? Would I subject you to danger, you, an actor, would I do anything to hurt you?' This is a man who will not brook no for an answer and probably seldom, if ever, hears that word. I tell him I will do anything that any actor can do but will not risk my flesh for an effect and quote the precautions, grease etc. The crowd round the set draw nearer and I sense the plump director's assistant uncomfortably near as if they were all voyeurs at a street accident.

'Out! Out! Out!' screams Mr Silver and they scatter like

The Explosion!

vultures feeding on a cadaver interrupted by an angry lion, which in itself is a marvellous effect and one cannot help but admire the sheer *chutzpah* of this man. He then goes into hyperdrive where he bobs and weaves and blasts a quick résumé of his films and grosses, discovering Eddie Murphy in the process and all this pouring out like a stream of consciousness and ending with, 'I need this shot.' His persuasive powers and performance made me relent and I okay'd it but I felt also that somewhere this nightmare must end. Just get through it. Charlie the stuntman whispers, 'You know you don't *have* to do it' and this remark rekindles my concern since he might have said, 'It's really nothing.' But Joel again comes up and offers to be in the shot with me but off-camera. Even my wardrobe man, Victor, looks at me with a tinge of sorrow.

I go back on the set and as I stand there I feel something cool on my neck. I am already being rubbed down like an animal being prepared for sacrifice. I turn and take the jar from the fireman and apply a liberal dose to my face, eyelids and wherever its protective shield of grease will go. I remember to rub it over my ears and hands. I remind Charlie of the stuntwoman rushed to hospital with second-degree burns: 'She didn't oil up properly.' I utter a small vow to myself that if anything happens to me, blood will be shed. I have endured much on this movie and accept the psychological pain as part of the price you have to pay in order to be employed. But physical pain is not in my contract. Mental is enough. The make-up lady hands me a cup of 'blood' and she has kindly added a drop of honey in it to take away the bitter taste. It all feels like a last rite and I am being sacrificed like a bull on the altar of the great temple to the god of movies, whoever that is.

We're ready. I do a dry acting run without the fire to show camera my exact position since this is a once-only shot. Joel says from his ringside seat, 'If it gets too hot, shout out and I'll stop it.' 'How am I to shout above the explosions?' I think. The set gets crowded on the edges and I note that the cameramen have covered all their equipment with blankets. I kneel down, having already been shot and hack away at the computer, trying to rescue my wealth once more. I think of the shark whose stomach has been cut open and yet still keeps eating its own innards. So this is me obsessed with my fortune as I bleed to death. I kneel and drink the stage blood with the honey in it as if it were the host. Smoke is poured into the hold of the ship where the HQ or code room is. It looks like the 'dinnest smoke of Hell'. 'Action' is called. I try to keep my face away from the fire and towards the camera lest my eyeballs melt. I am in a state of deadly calm. No fear. Just I couldn't care less. I am banging away at the keyboard, while leaking and spurting blood from my mouth. And then the first explosion goes off and then another and then another but so concentrated am I that the acting takes over and I feel nothing and hear little as if it was all a long way away.

I must have concentrated my mind into a trance. When I watched with Charlie, the stunt arranger, I was a spectator and of course felt it more. Being in the scene it was just a blast. Cut. Everybody claps since the whole thing must have looked impressive. It's over. Not quite. Now Joel wants the same thing again but this time with 500 gallons of water poured over me at the same time! What is this? Some kind of torture. Of course I did it but that is another story...

15
LA Story

19 August

I'm back here to dub *Fair Game*, the action film that I had the distinct misfortune to choose. You don't really have too much of a choice. Take it or don't work. It sounded as if it might be idyllic: two months in Miami and there were some beautiful days when the odoriferous nature of the work could be washed off in an azure sea but the rest of the time was devoted to making the lives of the actors Hell on earth since the novice director had a peculiar aversion for anything human. Chewing-gum dialogue, comic-strip plots, and the dehumanising or moronising of America. Somehow I got through it and fled from creatures that would make the inmates of Broadmoor seem like reasonable creatures.

A few months later I am dragged back to dub my Russian accent into 'British'! Some questionnaires filled in by the test audience were of the opinion that Russian villains were *old hat* and the studio supremos ignore the 'informed opinions' of the mob at their peril. This is a reasonable point of view since even idiots have opinions about the taste of their hamburger movies. However, this might have been thought of before we shot any of this masterpiece. So now I am seen trying to fit an English accent on to flamboyant Russian gestures since the studio bosses don't seem to make any distinction between races and dialects and ignore the inconvenient facts of different body language and different lip movement. Technology allows you to erase anything and fake everything. Now it looks and sounds like the voices that they put on chimpanzees in the commercials. Slowly, piece by piece, the old natural organic colour was drained away and my artificial studio voice was shoved over my image like a bad skin graft. Russians speak more slowly than the uptight Brit, relishing the language and the vowels and so, in order to match the lips' movements, I must speak slowly, and in English it sounds as if I am drugged or lobotomised. However ridiculous this sounds, one can only gasp in admiration at the sheer depth of their collective inanity. It is a bottomless pit. A black-hole that sucks in intelligence, wit, life, civilisation and art into its lifeless craw and even time is frozen. As I dub the 'dialogue' (for want of a better description) I become party to the destruction.

Since I did not readily acquiesce in what I thought was an act of madness, it was deemed necessary to force me with threats of blackmail in the ugly and familiar shape of litigation. 'Do it or be sued for everything you've got!' My lawyers thought I had a 'moral' case but in the end I decided to do the thing and get rid of it. It was painful, as during take after take if you missed the lip move by even a macro-second it would be enough to jar the eye, and so again and yet again, until there was no chance of any 'acting' but just a desperate race against the silently moving lips.

As the pain increased, the worthlessness of the exercise soured my brain and my perpetrators became evil tyrants whose images I would smash in my imagination. I would see Scarfe-like cartoons of myself vomiting up the trash in a big steaming evacuation which, on hitting the floor, would splosh into words making the title of the film. I would conjure up the fat producer pulling up his pants after wiping his arse on his devoted staff who stand there with giant rail tracks over their faces and bodies. Eventually, I escaped to my yuppie hotel on Santa Monica beach where fires glow over artificial logs and soft-bellied yuppies sit on the ample sofas with their legs folded under them almost as if they were home. My only relief is to take an evening stroll on Venice Beach, a beachside community that founded itself with the beats of the Fifties and Sixties and is still a haven for the mad, deranged, homeless deadbeats and me.

Early mornings are quite stunning – drenched in a rosy pink – and the hills of Santa Monica shimmer in the distance under a blue haze. The 'dead' crawl out of their blankets on the beach, stir from their special corner in the car parks which they protect as if it were real estate, rouse themselves from every corner, crevice, garage, garden, back porch, alleyway, until a small army of the dispossessed are seen straggling along Venice Beach. Apparently, Jack-the-Ripper Reagan is largely to blame for slashing so deeply into welfare that half the mental homes had to release their patients who tumbled out like disembowelled guts. Now we are able to enjoy the antics of the loonies from our sidewalk cafés, much like the audiences who travelled to Charenton to see the Marquis de Sade's lunatics act out his plays.

And now, even as I write, there are plans to close down two more local clinics in order to save money! More of the sick will drift down to the beach where there is a kind of sanctuary and they can beg some change. Others will perform acts too painful to behold as you eat your scrambled eggs and hash browns. As the waitress asks you, 'More coffee?' your head will swivel to take in an Amazonian beauty skimming past on her roller blades, sculptured to perfection and a picture of radiant health and as she leaves your picture frame, your eye is then caught by a figure in the background of a man half in and half out of a dustbin where he has been searching for treasure in the shape of old scraps of half-eaten pizza.

On my walk in the mornings I again pass the store where they hang out on the corner for meet-and-greet, grunting their way into the day, exchanging anecdotes, sitting on the benches with their polystyrene cups of coffee, acting just like normal folks at breakfast. They seem to have survived the need to emulate us normal folk and have a rawness and sinuousness which is enviable, their faces weathered, shaped and purged from that ever whingey look that characterises the worrying, petty bourgeoisie.

I like to sit at the café further down the boardwalk which caters to an early morning clientele that is one rung up from the hoboes. These tend to have flats nearby or sleep in ancient vehicles or vans parked perpetually in the lot. They all seem to know each other and greet with effusion. One or other has a dog which he doesn't like you to feed with your scraps. They seem to have a million things to talk about apart from what is going on in Venice and the conversation is passed back and forth over me as if I was a linesman at a tennis match. I'm invisible as they enter each other's lives and I have a strong desire to get to know them but I am from another planet, an alien so removed from anything here that I could not begin to cross their frontier.

I deeply envied their camaraderie, their morning café meetings, their confidence in meeting an ally each day, their hip jargon, their experience of the other side of America. I mourned the lack of such places in London where folk just meet and hang out and know each other, and expect to see each other. Back home it's a dreary 'each man for himself' and a peculiar lack of desire to fraternise. In London everyone's your enemy, fastening a fishy, glaucous eye on your existence and spitting at it from time to time. London seems to become increasingly petty and deeply conventional again as if, now that the radicals from the Sixties have died off, the more conservative can come out of their holes, sneer at each other (their favourite pastime) or choke to death on their Sunday papers. Here one has the relief on Sundays of having to read just the one grotty *LA Times* although it has to be the worst paper on Earth and you search it in vain for news of any kind. As you lift it up, pages of ad mags fall out like scurf which you shove into a bin. The other pages are giant ads with a hem of news clinging to the sides for dear life.

Don't spoil it with such thoughts, for now the sun pours down over our magic land of Venice where the hippies, and before them the Beats, made their home. There is some samba music playing and in one of the small bandstands the intoxicating sound is pouring out from a giant cassette and couples are dancing and inspired into some brilliant moves. Suddenly I am hungry to dance. I watch in envy as a guy is whipping his lithe female around as if she was a matador's cape. She seems weightless and curiously he is using the arm movements of jive while the feet are doing the samba which works very well. I feel I could do as well since this guy is dancing with an almighty smirk of satisfaction stitched to his face ('Ain't I the greatest thing?') and doing too many hand jive moves which has her relentlessly spinning although I have to admit that some are quite inventive.

(Flashback. Lyceum – The Fifties: We would spend hours trying out new and complex movements to see just how many ways there were of turning your partner and twisting her around you, of draping her arm around your neck and it was as elegant as the best rope artists; every permutation was tried and the more daring and original the better. It became your life, your style, what you were, how witty you could be, it reflected your coolness, your intelligence and body poetry. Also, a woman could always trust a dancer! Who said tough guys don't dance? Was it Norman Mailer?)

I watch the dancers one more time and the guy is now bamboozling another slim, pretty Latino with 'Ain't I smart?' moves and wearing that sickly eggy face as if he was the greatest thing on earth. I long to dance and show them that there is life in the old dog yet. Your energies, desires, longings, have not diminished that much but then she sees something else. She sees the opposite of what you see because your vision is interior. What she sees is an old man in her young eyes, an old man with silver-grey hair, cropped real short to give an impression of hard-edged youth, a raddled face where the shadows have cut even deeper grooves, a watery stare and an uncertain request for a dance. Fortunately, she spared your attempt to relive your fantasy which would have been, in reality, your humiliation. The old man waddles away down the boardwalk still mumbling in his thoughts of how wonderful he was...

The sun poured down and the crowds, as if bacteria, multiplied in the heat and now were a dense mass of seething flesh, anxious for their treats on this most florid of Sundays. Queues were long for the slices of pizza and burgers and bright-eyed servers were excited by the never-ending flow of money from an inexhaustible spring and were working with feverish intensity. Crowds quickly bloomed around any street performer worth his salt and soon he was playing to up to a hundred or more people. I became a part of the crowd, peeking in and admiring the real theatre where you would go out and strut your stuff and get paid *afterwards*. The street performer has to hold you or you just move on They don't go on drunk and wing it to a captive audience who are too ashamed to get up and flee. Here they are the fittest, with lightning reflexes, spontaneous reactors, sharp improvisers, elegant mimes. I watch and envy and now I want to be a street artist. To get up in Venice and do my stuff and I have hit on a brilliant idea for it but dare not reveal it right now. One day I will do it, for I see myself ending up on the boardwalk like a modern version of *Les Enfants du Paradis* with a little bucket for their change and happily spending my declining years here, where I will have no vindictive critics to scourge me. Here the audience are my critics and always have been.

Meanwhile, I look as these darting, brilliant, young, black

performers strut their talents and, Lo and behold! as I stand holding my hired cycle, one of them appears to recognise me and shouts out the name of a character I played in a movie. No name is as well known to the black public as that one in the whole lexicon of film history. I have had it shouted at me from passing cars, while walking along Venice boardwalk, sitting in airports, having breakfast at the Sidewalk Café while two guys jog past shouting it out. I am amazed that no one made a special movie on the character. *Victor Maitland*! I died in the first film and therefore he can't be revived. Meanwhile I smirk, shake my head as if he made the wrong identity and slink off sheepishly before the crowd start to wonder who I am. Like Poe's character who wanders the streets 'a man of the crowd', I am once more engulfed by the throng that swallows me, like Jonah, in its huge belly.

I drift and am carried along the currents of the great tide of humanity, out to enjoy and taste with every element of their being, to be startled, amused, excited, fed, pandered to, aroused, stimulated and entertained. Suddenly I see a small crowd gathering outside a clothes store and immediately see the object of their fascination. Two models are standing deathly still on a platform slightly above the crowd, displaying some of the store items. They are both perfectly formed, handsome, well-built, honed, streamlined, looking like movie stars, but the difference is that the two of them are human dummies. A light wind rustles through their fine blonde hair as they remain immobile as Greek statuary, indifferent to some of the crowd's yobbish elements whose own ordinariness provokes them to defensive jeers. The man looks like Robert Redford and almost seems to be bearing his extraordinary good looks with the disposition of one for whom to be so handsome is a cross to bear. The girl looks as if she has been formed and shaped by the best Nautilus machines and also wears an expression of disdain, but not too overtly, since they must tempt the customers. I am tempted and stare at them with naked admiration while at the same time I am greedily attracted to the waistcoat he is wearing. After a while the two warm-blooded statues have their break and I wander inside the store trying on waistcoats but eventually decide on the brocade waistcoat worn by the model, as if, subconsciously, I am craving to be like him. I pose in front of the mirror hoping somehow for the transformation and possibly some alchemical reaction is taking place: I drift out having allowed them to rub my plastic card which allows me rather more than three wishes as long as you can afford them.

I am relieved to be in the air again as if each penetration into a store was a symbolic onanistic act, which in a way it is. Now waistcoated, I push further down the boardwalk where the beach area gives way to an extended path and another small crowd gathers around the skaters who are mostly of black origin with one or two white fellow travellers and a couple of tarty-looking chicks who are the groupies of a very flash dude I have been watching for years and is another one of these mythic figures that dot my life – people who are untouchable and unknowable as if they have achieved a kind of immortality for doing something that mere mortals cannot. When I first saw him, he had the most incredible physique, narrow-waisted, washboard abs, snakes writhed through his biceps and shoulders. He used to wear a unique cap which had two horns sewn in the top and which seemed appropriate, while he skated like a dream and when he spoke, sounded like Paul Robeson. Now all this is *très* selfconscious since you are skating for the crowd of mere sub-humans and tourists. He fools, jousts, plays, dances, forms small combos with other like-minded skaters as if he was a dance teacher in a private academy, while surrounding him were all the smaller fishes spinning round, making pirouettes on the four wheels. The master devil just circled his small concrete domain like a shark in a giant fish tank.

I have this desire to make contact with unusual people, just a touch, a gesture of wanting a brief admittance to their club but could never do so with him. I photographed him dozens of times all through the years and it became such that Venice would not have been the same for me without him. This strange and exotic beast would be a gargoyle if Venice was a cathedral. But he is always here, year after year, gliding around on his four-wheeled skates, chatting up all the women and giving them familiar, teacherly but sexual hugs, laughing and making his big voice resound, taking off again for no particular purpose but to feel weightless. There he was today and, as usual, I have this terrible urge to make some exchange but am relegated to the fringes who just stare at this sacred ground where the bacchae romp and play. Today he hasn't the skates on but still likes to move selfconsciously to the music as he raps to his chum. All watch with the squinty, small, sun-starved eyes of Europe and, not wishing to feel like this, I moved on into the crowd and decided to take a coffee in the little open-air café round the corner.

As I arrive I bump into my old film colleague Voyo, who played the 'heavy' in *Rambo II* and who fights to the death with Stallone in the film. Now, ten years have passed and still he has that brazen, huge, Yugoslavian presence that so annoyed the great Sly that the star wanted to get rid of him and, on that occasion, I was able to placate him and act as Lenny in *Mice and Men* and look after my brute. He was still big and powerful-looking but perhaps has melted down a bit over the years. His hair shoots out of his skull like flames and he is with his dog whom he loves. We sit and the late afternoon sun makes us surrender to the charms of the past when we would rent a jeep in Mexico's playground Acapulco and just drive and drive, happy to be anywhere but that set with all its confabulations and plots. We'd drive to tiny Mexican villages where all the kids would come out to see the giant and stare at him with brown eyes, in wonder that anything could be so huge, and then at night he would score with a 'chicita' who was equally fascinated by the man-monster, and wished to try it out. The full report would be given by Voyo the next day with sound effects, mime and assorted gestures. He wants to work but has none since he can only play what his accent and skills permit and so he is taking some acting classes. I suggest he looks at Eugene O'Neill's great play *The Hairy Ape* and learn the part of Yank. I love this play and have always wanted to play it but now I have passed the time limit on this one too, I guess. He writes it down. The part of Yank. His eyes are almost closed as if he concentrates on getting his ample personality out that seems hidden inside this torso. A good, sensitive human being still looking for what he is in America. He disappears into the crowd which swallows him in one gulp. I just see the last of his hair going down the gullet.

The sun is now sinking over the hills of Malibu and the crowds are streaming from the beaches as the car parks are thinning out and the pizza stand man is counting his huge wad of money. I like this time of evening to sit and watch the deepening of the sky as it goes from blue to deep flushy red, whorishly making up for the night's escapades and so I wander over to the Sidewalk Café and sink a margarita. The café is quite crowded as this is a popular spot for the spectacular sunset and to view the late evening roller bladers and assorted eccentrics that drift past providing such amusement for the diners. Like a menagerie of differing malfunctions, the inmates of Venice walk up and down, bumming a cigarette or some change from the customers and even occasionally berating and abusing them.

As I drink and salute the spectacular moving painting in the sky I am joined by a British colleague, David, a painter who has succeeded in working out here for over a dozen years and is now part of the exotic embroidery of the Venice character. Either you embrace it and be absorbed into its weft, or forever stand outside like a curious tourist fascinated and somewhat drawn, wishing to return to the freedom of childhood for a few days before flying back to the oppressive regime of adulthood in Munich or London. David is a reformed alcoholic and goes to AA meetings. He took me once as an observer but in order to be admitted I had to say, 'My name is Steven, I'm an alcoholic.' It felt strange saying it but I suppose in some way I could be since I have had a drink every night for years now and it seems to go with my daily ritual.

David leaves and I walk back through the crowds and disappear into the distance until I am just a spot in the landscape.

16
A Face in the Crowd

Monday 2 September

It is going to be a gorgeous, hot, burning, blue day and the Venice boardwalk right up to Santa Monica pier is exploding as usual with black energy, wit, power, elegance, great physical beauty and vivacity. It is early morning and the alternative gunge that feed on the idle curiosity of tourists are already setting up their tables as fortune tellers, tarot card readers, massage benches and the like. The air is still a silvery grey before the sun has burnt through and so I crawled out of bed with the expectancy I always have here of what mysteries will unfold and I wrap the early morning around myself as I run down to the public outdoor gym near the pier. I wonder how many times and for how many years I have done this, and for how many years I will continue to do so, until the hips can no longer swivel in their sockets when I walk and maybe when I can no longer walk. Then I will stare from the hotel that I have been staying at, on and off, for fifteen years!

Yet when I am running it seems as if I have been here for ever and the gap between the last time miraculously shortens like it was only days before and not a year or two. The mornings here have that distinctive aroma which I find so attractive, a Venice perfume which is unlike any other – a mixture of the hills of Santa Monica, sea, gasoline and disinfectant – a heavy pungent odour and the girls smell like candy floss. So I run past the Pritiken Institute, that hallowed institution where the overweight sacrifice their fat and dollars, and reach the sandy area where there are a few parallel bars of varying heights plus a pull-up bar, no fan of that, and sweating gently, do twenty or thirty dips but in three sets and sharply recall the familiar, cold touch of the steel poles ploughing into my palms. After my few proud exertions I can walk back calmly, feeling I have accomplished something.

The sun is now facing and warming me. I pick up a coffee at one of the beach cafés where the homeless have already gathered for their early morning ritual, having crawled out of their ragged filthy cocoons and are sipping slowly on their first hit of caffeine. As it is now 8 o'clock I enter the famous Sidewalk Café, my ritual breakfast diner since 1980 when I first came here like Paris seeking Helen. The café is celebrating its twentieth anniversary since it opened, having reclaimed some of the derelict property that was the remains of ancient Venice reproduced here, hence the name Venice Beach. It was a beautiful idea in the Twenties but slowly fell into dilapidation and the great promenades were pulled down and the columns crumbled but some remained and they are still here at the Sidewalk Café with their gargoyles.

I sat right at the far end so that no one could sit behind me and, as I have done so many times before, I observed the world passing. The waitress looked a bit put out at having to walk the length of the café and so she couldn't resist detonating her frustration by announcing, 'You made me walk to the end!' I retaliated swiftly since I had already absorbed her sour look from a distance and didn't wish to accept her terms of the joke. I pretended to take it seriously and opted to change seats if it suited her, at which remark her sour face tried to unpuke itself and she retorted that she was only joking. I wanted my special delicacy of granola and fruit for breakfast but apparently couldn't have it since, 'We don't do it on the weekend, but only on weekdays!' Yankees love rules, but I compromised by having a separate dish of fruit to go with my granola. Terrific. It tasted marvellous as anything would in the cool, silvery, early morning air, as I sat outside watching the Venetians sliding past. I absorb the strange world out here, fascinated with the weirdos, the beggars, the down-and-outs, the homeless, the drifters, the skaters, the joggers, the walkers, the dog walkers, the ones going to the gym, the muscly ones, the ancient ones... It tasted so good that I celebrated the event by taking a couple of photos of the café and the early morning eaters with my Nikon.

On the weekend it's a parade out here. A stream of exotic fish of every variety in the world, and so apart from the bums and the joggers, are the white, strutting slobs, reversed-baseball caps, guys with brilliantly-hued parrots that will pose on your shoulder for a $5 photo; Mas and Pas walking around with open mouths who become the targets of swift-speaking sardonic black comics. There are performance artists with full Artaudian front displaying a fearless dynamic that cannot help but pull in the crowd who stand agape, hoping not to be picked on as the butt for their humour but, once they are, seeming to take it all in good fun and actually quite liking it in a perverse sort of way. A young man with a huge python wrapped around him is taking a walk just like he was walking a dog. The sun is coming strongly through and I gulp in the air like it was precious. I am in fantasy land and liberated from the shackles of my old being and culture, for here is anarchy and circus, frivolity and space in which to be frivolous. I notice the menu at the Sidewalk Café announces a special offer; that on anniversary day all prices will be the same as they were in 1980! Boy, it will be packed on 18 September! I read through the grimly dull *LA Times* and am hooked on the sad and terrible story of a family who were slain in their trailer by giving hospitality to some strangers...

The English manageress comes by and we have a rare chat and I tell her, as I did the waitress, that I have been coming here for fifteen years. Her name is Tricia and she tells me that she is the sister of the other plump manageress. These two Brits manage the best, the most interesting and well-run café-diner in LA. We chatter and dredge up the past, commenting on this one and that one whom we might have mutually known from the café, like old regulars and waitresses. I ask about Diane, a beautiful, thick-haired waitress whom I was sweet on for a while and it transpired that she has taken off and is raising a family somewhere in the South. They cannot be in the café forever, returning as I do but must go on evolving their lives. A black guy with a shaved head bangs on a garbage bin pretending it's his drum while appearing out of his mind, which is not unusual round here. He accompanies his thwacks with shouts. Meanwhile sitting on a bench with his pet raven is a guy who claims he found the poor little creature looking worn out and forlorn in his back yard and yet the guy clipped its wings and now you can see the stumps like the ends of mutilated fingers. The owner of the bird justifies his mutilation, saying that the bird would otherwise be attacked by other birds since it was out of its territory or some such rubbish but the creature seems happy with all the attention it is getting from people who come over and say, 'Can I hold him?'

I strolled to the table tennis court, passing the clown with the white face who makes animals out of balloons having his breakfast just like other normal folk while things were still quiet. As I arrived at the court, I saw that my partner Barry was already there, moaning that all the courts were full and so they were since it was Labour Day and on most courts people were forced to play doubles.

Being in Venice makes you feel like you belong to one huge

family since it is a city in microcosm except everything is at your fingertips and it is also a fool's playground where you never really have to grow up. Barry played Eddie years ago in my play *Greek* and was exceptionally good and therefore got no work since there are few possibilities for excellent working-class actors. So he flew to the land of opportunity but found it difficult here too and drifted away from a brilliant future. He has a couple of tennis rackets and we deposited them in the corner of an occupied court just as a marker that we were the next in line. We then watched over the court possessively as the guys played out their last points. At the end they introduced themselves and I marvel at their sheer sociability until I realise their apparent friendliness is motivated more by the desire to keep on playing. One informs us that since it is a holiday we are obliged to play doubles which will be a killer for rank amateurs, since these guys are regulars. I didn't think of questioning why they had been playing singles quite contentedly and that we should have the same opportunity for at least a set and *then* play doubles but we are so overcome by their 'Hi, guys' and 'My name is' that we didn't think clearly.

Barry and I warmed up on one side of the court banging the ball backwards and forwards and trying to look as if we might be formidable opponents after all. However, while they gave us both a sound thrashing they also gave us a much needed lesson at the same time. We were humiliated in double-quick time and could barely get a sweat up, before their real partners came and we were deprived of our game while those bastards went on to play for a third time. As we passed the courts I noticed a strange creature whom I have seen play there before. She looked like something out of an old touring production of *Sunset Boulevard*, a ghostly-looking female of about sixty although she could even be ninety, thin as a weed like she was anorexic; her match-stick legs were covered in lacy tights and net leotard plus her face was painted as if she was in a Kabuki play. Yet she managed to hold the bat firmly and hit the ball.

On a mate's Harley in Sydney. I actually did ride it round the block!

Above: Roller-blader descending against backdrop of Bondi Beach.
Below: Bondi Beach. Life-saver with white lipstick.
Below, inset: Hanging out in Bondi Beach.

Above: Copacabana Beach – Rio.
Above, inset: Myself and actor Peter Firth on prior excursion to Rio.
Below: 'Picturesque' slums in backstreet Rio.

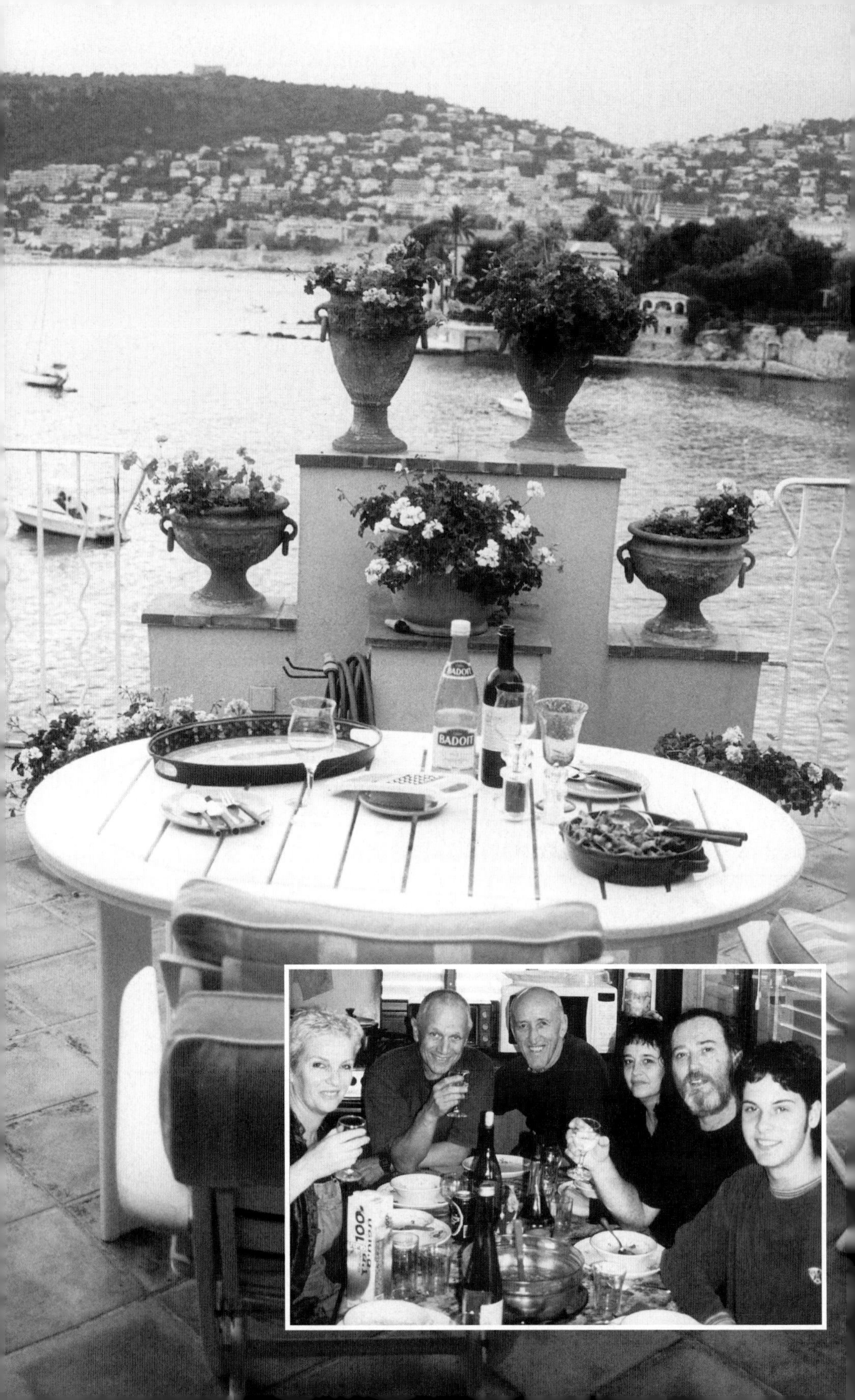
BADOIT
BADOIT

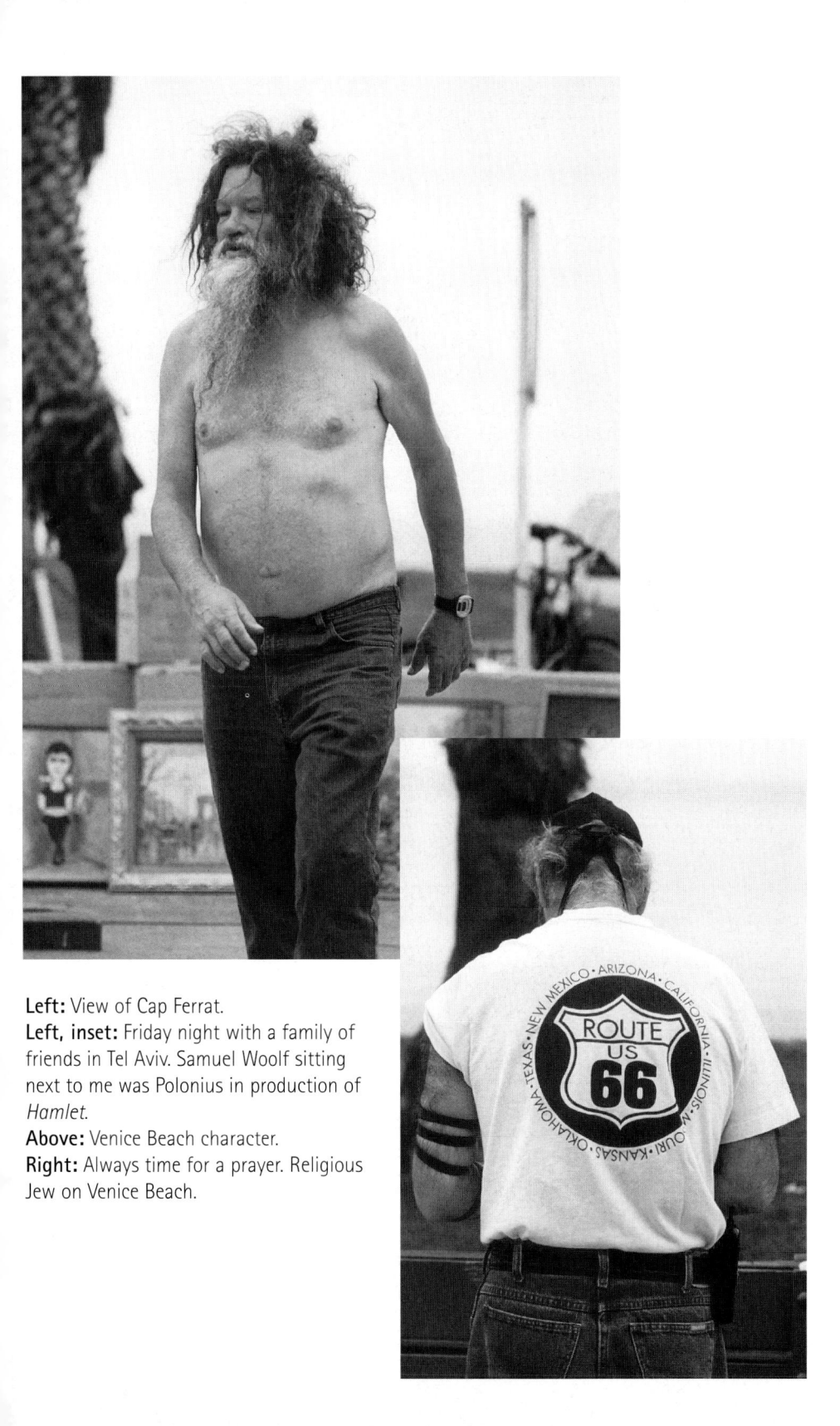

Left: View of Cap Ferrat.
Left, inset: Friday night with a family of friends in Tel Aviv. Samuel Woolf sitting next to me was Polonius in production of *Hamlet*.
Above: Venice Beach character.
Right: Always time for a prayer. Religious Jew on Venice Beach.

Above, top: Venice Beach. Anyway, it's home.
Left: Flower power still exists on Venice Beach.
Above: 'Buddy, can you spare a dime?' Homeless on Venice Beach.

Left: Venice Beach. Fortune teller with 'nails'.
Below: 'Sexy' granny on the Venice Beach Boardwalk, Los Angeles.

Right: 'Piss in the Sink Productions'. *Brighton Beach Scumbags* – armed with giant quiff.
Below: Me and Tony Curtis in Palm Springs for première of my first movie, *Decadence*.
Bottom left: *Decadence*. Joan Collins and her very proud director/actor.
Bottom right: Joan and I in *Decadence*.

This is the American dream turned into a *Baby Jane* nightmare of Gothic horror and could only be an aspect of LA since this place breeds the ghouls who were once pretty and have tried to freeze-dry their looks.

The sun poured down upon the little run-down patio of the Israeli café and the stream of people coming down to the beach for Labour Day was steadily thickening the boardwalk with young and eager flesh. Barry has to work in the part-time job he has in catering. He helps to set up barbecues in the private houses and gardens of the rich. Of course the rich and famous don't really notice the staff and since they are in no way in either fear of them or respect for them but see them merely as tools with arms they are inclined to be more 'natural'. Barry told me of one famous, short, fat actor who hovered greedily saying, 'Gimme this and gimme that' and ate it like a starving pig at a trough. Got to be careful how you behave in public for doesn't Hamlet say that 'actors are the brief chronicles of the time' or words to that effect? So are waiters!

We left shortly after and I unaccountably found myself drawn back to the flowing swell of humanity, its intoxicating mix and the sights and smells of the Venice boardwalk.

Around various street acts are clumps of people, clusters of eager faces in a semicircle circle like metal filings around a magnet or perhaps like dozens of moons surrounding a planet or they may even be like planets being warmed by the sun. These guys are some of the most inventive performers it has been my privilege to watch, to envy, to wish to be, to express the ultimate act of street theatre.

Then I saw Ruben with his hair cut into a flat top, which resembles a garden hedge immaculately trimmed. A veritable topiarist, forsooth! Ruben has turned his entire body into one of those marvellous high-tech toys that can swivel in all directions. His structure is a work of art, he can appear to elongate his shape at will, curving his body backwards as if made of plasticine. He has perfected his video-style art, performs an action miming it perfectly with freeze-frame authenticity, moving a small section of his body at a time and then he appears to malfunction and keeps repeating the action which is hysterically funny. He performs a simple human movement, like greeting a friend with a smile which is then wiped off and then appears again as if the creature is forever stuck and cannot go forwards in time. He is the embodiment of street art. He is a poet in space and while his body is an incredible instrument it is aided by the joyous frenzy which he gives out in his robot man. In our techno-video age it is the street which picks up first the desire to mock, emulate and satirise while the old narcissists are still dripping oily tears over old revivals where all the bodies wearily and drearily drag their utterly drab carcasses round the stage. He wears a deep blue kind of zoot suit and looks radiant, glossy with the moisture of his exertions.

I wish to be able to perform these stunts, these plastic, liquid, pneumatic, robotic movements and I watch him carefully until he gathers up his money when the act is over. I then congratulate him as I always do. He seems pleased to see me as if I was a fan going backstage. I beg him to teach, to put a sign up offering his secrets of body motion, to make a pot of cash. He likes the idea but he doesn't believe that he can teach it since it comes so naturally to him he wouldn't be able to break it down. Now he's ready to begin again and I wander over to the next group.

I move around fonts of energy, to warm myself at the glow, to be inspired and affected. There is a huge crush of people gathered round the next powerhouse performer, a Frenchman whom I have seen many times before and so I pass on. At the end of the boardwalk is a film crew shooting a sequence since this is the most popular place for filming and most people here are so inured to it they pay little attention. I recognise an actor in it (quite well known) standing on his spot waiting for the cameras to roll when he moves through the crowd apparently in pursuit of someone. Two of the leads are playing cops on bikes, the kind of wholesome cute cops in shorts and white socks that you see riding around Venice. Both players look sickeningly perfect in that homogenised, plasticy, healthy, trimmed and trained way, which anyway is a change from the pasty, spotty, blotchy, night-after, British look much favoured until the likes of Daniel Day-Lewis came around. The American guy is so handsome he looks a little embalmed.

I pass on and glance into one of those narrow passageways that link the rear ends of buildings where they put out the garbage and which usually carries the distinctive whiff of evacuated liquid deposits. It links Pacific Avenue and the boardwalk. It's a dark, sunless alleyway. As I look into the gloom adjusting my eyes after the blinding beauty of the beasts on bikes, I noticed an old black guy (or he seems old) rising from one of the doorways. I am compelled to stare at him as if trying to quantify our differences and then try to justify myself. He blinks back as he rises from his rat-infested squalor and tries to show me he is human and the contrast, between what I have just beheld on the boardwalk and this, is just too obscene.

I walked back to the circles of energy that I had passed before and the magnet there is the Frenchman called David Allen. He invents daringly and brilliantly on the spot using the audience for his material and is most admired by the audience for his endearingly cheeky habit of impersonating innocent passers-by whom he cruelly mimics from behind as he satirises their walk. The 'victim' is at first unaware of what is happening but gradually it dawns on them through the laughter that something untoward is happening and they turn around and all they see is a strange-looking gaunt man looking perfectly innocent.

Now he is cleverly using children and such is the public's trust of performers that they allow him to use them as props. He puts a dollar equidistant between two tiny kids of about five years old and has them race for the precious note. In this case the crowd roars as the little girl speeds to it while the little boy hardly makes an effort. This could be a scientific test on the early programming of children's minds. Then he takes a baby from a pram and offers it a milk bottle from the one hand and a dollar bill in the other. The baby is still natural and goes for the milk bottle each time which has the crowd roaring again. The entertainment is almost Elizabethan. He borrows kids from different families, takes two strangers and gives the infants to them to hold as if he was giving them away and then with someone else's camera he takes a picture of the instant family. It's a testament to his skill that he is able to do anything to you and use you merely as the clay he fashions his mini-dramas from. He has the touch of a Svengali, guru, master, magician. He is also smart by using his own dollars for bait. He finished and once he turns off the juice the crowd disappears and he returns them to the flowing stream to become anonymous bobbing heads once more. For a while they were part of him and he of them, for a few moments a little society, as of course all audiences are. I learned his name when I spoke to him and he told me he had worked with Marcel Marceau, the great one. He told me he does an act in Santa Monica Mall which has become quite an area for performance artists and that I should see him there and I promised that I would.

I then splintered away and was attracted further down the boardwalk by two extraordinary black comic acrobats. They both wore matching striped pants and spoke almost as one just like they have been working together for years and have perfected their act. They were doing the latest thing which is to charmingly tread on the hot coals of political correctness and come away unscathed. They demonstrated a white man dancing and then a black man dancing and used the crowd as examples and what they did was to melt down not only the differences between black and white but to make these very differences a source of charm and fascination while at the same time appearing to be very bold with stereotypes. So they took a white, dopey-looking guy out of the audience who is usually chosen because he represents the typical goon with shorts, reversed baseball cap and sheepish grin. Then they turn on the tape and execute a few really cool dance moves that they ask honky to reproduce which he does of course like a farmyard yokel! The crowd laughs at being sent up and to have a scapegoat to take the heat off them. The two black guys now increase the stakes and looking slim and athletic begin now to impersonate how the white man has danced and portray him as thick, gormless, unmusical, without rhythm and graceless but they are so charming about it that the crowd fall about in rapture while the goon seems happy to be, for the first time in his life, the centre of attention. Now in his euphoric state the white guy/victim is grinding his hips which not only looks revolting but acutely embarrassing and he seems to be indulging in his own pathetic grotesqueness as if to say, 'Well, this is me, folks.' Fortunately they cut him off and conclude with a series of acrobatic dance steps and finally beg for dollars with what I thought was just a little too much brio as even in this they are so cute.

I lurch off into the stream letting myself be carried whichever way. I become a face in the crowd carried by its flow, drifting to the next destination where I will pause for a while to catch my breath, always a moon, dipping and weaving in the crowd.

17
Another Deli – Wolfies in Miami

Of course there's nothing like it on Earth, it's the equivalent of the elephant graveyard for the Jews of Miami and has been here since 1947. The faithful come for that familiar smell and taste of home and the deli is unique in that it unifies all. Jews from every part that were scattered like so much seed on the wind reunite in the Promised Land of the deli where every taste of Mom will be satisfied. Since I was here a couple of years ago Wolfies seems to have faded somewhat since the young and middle-class have not the same cravings as their parents for the familiar aroma of shtetel, ghetto and slum and go to fancy white-walled Italian galleries where food is served, like a painting, with a twist of complementing colour and sharp-tasting, chilled wines from cool, dark cellars. Here food is served like a feast for carnivores: obscenely huge corned beef sandwiches cut in half revealing their great wedges of dull, pinkish meat held together by thin, soggy slices of rye bread, steam rising from the sandwich's guts like it had just been ripped out of a recently slaughtered animal. So you try to soften the impact by a little deflection of mustard, then ram in some pickle, squash the tile of bread back on the roof of beef and open your mouth for a terrific crunch. A bowl of soggy pickles sits on the table.

It is, like much of Miami, constructed in art deco style to go with the paint-blue skies and velvet green of the local vegetation, pinky-rose dawns and purple sunsets. The counter is pastel green surrounded by deeper apple-green bar stools that sit like mushrooms atop strawberry pink stands. The chairs surrounding the small tables are in two-tone pink and green. The large booths against the wall are a dirty pink from wear. The ceilings in America are not thought to be very important – since who looks at the ceiling? – which are tiled in that familiar cream that is now carrying the stains of decades of diners whose breath, smoke, smell and heat has forever imprinted itself like nicotine stains on the fingers of a smoker. The corners of the squares, like stale corners of sandwiches, are beginning to curl up in agony. Maybe Wolfies comes to life at night like Cantors in LA but during the day it is the deli for passing trade and for a large swathe of Miami's community of Jews, the older ones who have traipsed here for years, ancient crocks bent over like hairpins escorted by an equally ancient crock or a black maid. The old one is somehow indelibly the last vestige of ghetto life, a body that battles valiantly against the debilitating effects of a youthful diet steeped in schmaltz and lack of exercise and a devotion to the soul food of chopped liver and eggs, wurst and fatty chicken soup with lots of cheesecake. Nevertheless she carries her racked, old body like a faithful adherent to Wolfies where she will relive the atmosphere of the kitchen table and the music of the chattering Jewish tongue.

As if to order, as if to fulfil the stereotypical image which Israel has eradicated forever in its new breed of healthy and powerful Jews, we see here the manager waddle up and down, supporting his gargantuan girth, a veritable barrel, neckless, a round football for a head in which two dark eyes swivel as if they were the only really mobile part and could check the restaurant at far greater speeds than this huge girth could turn. It all seems to be part of the intense Yiddish past: stifling tenements, small rooms, smoking fires, screaming babies, dining tables surrounded by shouting card players and the escape into food, which is the balm, soothing and calming as the chicken soup assuages all ills.

The café staff seem as if picked from central casting and would-be extras in the TV series *The Munsters* and have the slick, world weary, cynical air of working in a place where the food never changes; they cannot become creatively excited like a waiter in the Italian theatre of food who learns his 'specials' like an aria for the day while singing the praises of a starter of arugula and razor-shaved Parmesan cheese resting like snow atop a salad doused in balsamic dressing. Here no such music will ever enter or leave his mouth. Only 'One corned beef and chicken soup' and 'Wadya wanna drink?!' He works a territory bereft of the demands of youth, in fact which youth avoids like a plague and where cynicism is the only safeguard against rejection and a lifetime's incarceration in schmaltz. There is an attitude of Yiddish cynicism based on hopelessness and 'you will never surprise me and so, what's new' since centuries of claustrophobic oppression cannot be wiped out overnight in air-conditioned apartments and wide avenues. It will gradually thin out with each generation but here it sits in a carefully preserved time warp. No glamour of Miami stops here, but crusty, creaky age, neurotic and obsessive needs, a body full of pills and now some nostalgia to wash it down. The manager is walking around with that strut that fat men have which makes them look a little important from where we get that expression 'Don't throw your weight around,' which is exactly what he can't help doing. His chin meets his chest which seems grateful to rest on it. His thick, black beard seems to add that touch of seriousness to the indulgence of blubber as if it might be begging some attention to its owner's mensch-like quality.

There has to be some absolutely determined reason why the

aged, the broken, the bulbous work these restaurants, apart from the sanctuary it offers our more nebbish brothers and sisters, for we do not have hard-bodied Italian waiters dancing around the tables, barely concealing their healthy glowing muscles beneath their crisp white shirts, nor cheeky pearly-white-toothed girls bursting with sexual vitality beneath their starched little white aprons. As the deli is a wonderful collection of the viands of history, a plaiting together of the tastes of ancient Europe into one coil of delicacy so doth it not also bring with it some element of the human past that seems to go with it, not that I want body builders and sexy babes taking the order for gefilte fish but I merely observe that for the real feeling of the Jewish deli we seem to have characters that have just stepped out of the Warsaw Ghetto.

True, I see one or two waitresses who come into view who are not so *tsukirochen* (tired-looking, a little worn) but now my waiter comes over. He is priceless and by no means is he Jewish either but once the mandatory style is absorbed you grow into the role. His gestures have become so perfunctory they have developed an almost ritualistic pattern. He flicks open his order book, speedily takes your order, 'Chicken soup, one coffee!' and snaps the book shut on the order like it was a lizard snapping shut its jaws on a tasty fly. He wears the traditional black waistcoat, white shirt and black pants, which apart from the shirt are stiff with the clues of his trade. In the same way the painter's smock contains elements of every painting he has executed in the years he has been wearing that particular smock, so this man's trousers and waistcoat must have the encrustations of several thousand plates of food. In other words, they were really crusty! After a few days or weeks it can't get any filthier, as Quentin Crisp so wisely observes in his philosophy about his apartment. We pretend not to notice as if it all fits in to the 'colour' and the 'charm' of the busy, tasty, eat-and-enjoy, deli. The pain of the past leaves a legacy, the eternal shrug of 'who cares' but I do care and I had the distinct pleasure of eating in a deli in LA recently that was a model of perfection combining great Jewish deli with the streamlining of the times we live in. But here it is still not so important. My waiter scuttles through the dining room like a black beetle and seems fleshless, like his hips have no arse on them and he is a collection of bones held together by parchment and the crusty waistcoat. His face registers just the faintest glimmerings of life and since it inspires even a little fear, I am excessively polite as if his filthy crustiness, his dead eyes, his obscene lack of flesh were combined to extract almost unwillingly some admiration. I mean, this is a being who lives in Hell!

My chicken soup arrives and tastes wonderful and hosts a matzo ball and noodles and is golden as it should be. But then I risked a corned beef sandwich, actually a half, allowed 'if you purchase a soup'. It came looking unpleasant, a thick pink slab rolled up and put between two half slices of bread. They had not made a whole sandwich, cut it in half and saved the other half for the next 'soup and half a sandwich', no, they had just grabbed a lump of meat and smacked the bread over it so it lacked that crisp, sharply cut edge that is part of the aesthetics of eating. I mean presentation is just as important as taste. It was steaming as if it had been microwaved and the bread was hot and gooey over what looked like some rather slimy meat, not helped by the fact that I never eat it except when some atavistic pull takes me to a Jewish deli. I didn't like the meat resembling the dusty pink booths of the restaurant. I took one nibble only and my whole being, tongue, nose, touch and sight concentrated into one gesture of repulsion. This was not the great sandwiches of Juniors of Brooklyn or even the great Katz deli in SoHo, New York or even Cantors in LA let alone the famous one in the Rue des Rosiers, Paris since I have tried them all already, tried them all. So I looked at the perpetual, art deco blue sky through the window to wash my mind clean of the horror. The crusty, fleshless waiter had gone and I felt for him but his image will remain indelibly fixed in my mind as happens when a place loses its joy and energy and slides downhill and becomes decayed. He was a touch Kafkaesque, perhaps a cousin to Gregor Samsa just before he became a beetle, and might be a candidate for such a metamorphosis. There is still a certain charm and a famous Jewish chutzpah about the endless menu. Yet it contains too many vestiges of the past and I was glad to escape to the fresh-painted, sharp-looking, youthful café on South Beach. I suppose I was also glad, years ago, to escape from the soupy confines of London's East End.

18
Palm Springs

Got through Customs at great speed and as I entered the concourse I was greeted by a uniformed driver who escorted me to a long, black limo which swallowed me in one gulp and whisked me off to Palm Springs. Flopping back in this mobile lounge I decided to try and get some sleep. 'Hey there's some drinks in the back, and some wadder, juz help yourself.' 'Okay, thanks.' I decided to take advantage of the offer, grabbed one of the decanters of what I thought was the 'wadder' but turned out to be some harsh alcoholic stew. I poured it back, dribbling some on my shirt in the process. One could observe that I was not used to this way of life. From a long shot the camera would see a long, black, funeral hearse cruising along the desert and, within, a single sardine rattling around emitting worrying, jet-lagged thoughts.

I got to the Spa Hotel in Palm Springs by 6 p.m. which was 2 a.m. my time (how we love to count the hours), had a bath and ripped open my new dress shirt (which seemed to spawn pins), shaved, found my black velvet jacket that I bought in Australia last year and was now very grateful for, slipped off my intelligent digital watch which stores phone numbers, acts as a calculator and performs many tasks and donned my second-hand Rolex, which isn't at all smart but looks all steel and chunky and emits symbolic manifestations of power for those who aren't sure of their own, went downstairs and waited in the bar for Lance Reynolds, my Australian producer of *Decadence* which was to be shown at the Palm Springs Film Festival the following day. I ordered a margarita and waited. There is that tingling feeling when you've just arrived in a foreign country and you're watching the inhabitants as if they were from another planet.

   The elderly lady who was working on the door wanders over in a quiet moment and chats to me, weaving a mini-history which was fascinating since it told how the 'Indian nation', as they are called, have bought this hotel with its natural springs and are revamping it and now plan to introduce gambling to Palm Springs for the first time. Since the times of Palm Springs's heyday, when it was *the* resort to go to, it has slid back and is losing out to the other 'desert' cities. Basically Palm Springs is two long main streets intersected with scores of cross-streets. It's a charming, innocent, curious, pleasant shop and café-lined environment nestling in the foothills and surrounded by one of the most beautiful landscapes. It is the home of the legends who slide down Mount Olympus in Beverly Hills, like the ancient pharaohs going to the desert to die, but here in this dry, warm environment you die slowly. Bob Hope and Frank Sinatra are amongst its more famous denizens. Everything is clean, sparkling and tasty and when the sun shines, as it mostly does, it's hot, blue-canopied, patch-worked with deep topaz-blue chlorinated pools festooned with Italian cafés like Banduccis, where you sit outside on the veranda, admire the stars and eat Yankee-style Italian fast foods.

   So the management says Palm Springs needs a revival and already I am struggling in my mind to see what I can do to save it since she seems to be sharing this agony with me and her half-empty hotel, manned by an indifferent hotel receptionist who welcomed me with less warmth than the mechanical voice on my fax machine. I can see what she means. I used to think of Palm Springs as a kind of American Delphi where, apart from the retired relics and gods of the screen, old millionaires would live a secluded life calmed by the gentle susurrus of the sprinkler on the manicured lawns. Medical perfection is what only private medicine can give you if you are rich enough and have insurance, but up yours, mister, and wait for hours in line in some poor state hospital if you haven't. Dan Quayle, the super-moron of American politics this very week, seeing himself in a hospital operating room, sang the virtues of private medicine, thus condemning at one stroke some 30 million Americans who have no insurance. However, it seems that brains and values are certainly not the prerequisite of Yankee politics.

Anyhow *Decadence*, my scorching excoriation of the sins of indulgence, is to have its première in the old Plaza Cinema, a beautiful, old, art deco cinema now lost, alas, for movies, as they have a ghastly multiplex round the corner, but it is still being used for what they call *Follies*, a stage show of theatrical twaddle so popular in these regions. I pick up the local *Desert Times* and scan it for any relevance to the modern world and one of the main news items in the culture section is the emerging from semi tomb-like retirement of two ancient and distinguished actresses to play in a piece aptly called *Legends* and for which these two had been rudely shaken out of their twilight zone. The photos of the two stare out hopefully, almost grateful to be given an opportunity to snatch with their broken talons a few more unexpected bouquets.

Lance and I climb into another dark, giant limo to take us across the road to where my old acting partner Tony Curtis is being celebrated. The front of the limo is almost there before we have hardly left, like Cyrano's celebrated nose that walks a mile ahead of him. We arrive and there is a gaggle of elderly people clutching their little flash cameras and they ignore me since they can't quite make me out: familiar but not HOUSEHOLD! As we enter the foyer we check on the board to see where our table is and the names surrounding the tables look like the list of actors currently playing in my video store: Arnold Schwarzenegger, Bob Hope, Ginger Rogers, Jamie Lee Curtis and Donald O'Connor, who partnered Gene Kelly in the great 'hoofer' movies, but by then we were ushered in to our table and arrived late but in time to see O'Connor host the occasion with great wit and timing and looking fit and strong for all his 70-plus years. Tony is being 'celebrated' since he never received any awards for a lifetime of service to the industry despite having hacked out a few more than good performances, and some considered brilliant, such as in *Some Like it Hot* and *The Sweet Smell of Success*. He is the bad boy of the industry, a kind of loose cannon who didn't mature into the stalwart, steely-grey rectitude of Lancaster and Douglas who earned their seats on Mount Olympus and immortality. Curtis still clings to the succulent sweets of this world being the heady delights of unlimited sensual gratification through both protuberances. They didn't come but send best wishes from Kirk Douglas, Frank Sinatra who only lives down the road, and Liz Taylor. Now Esther Williams, yes, the great Esther Williams is there and makes a speech which totally floors the audience with its wit and timing and candour of her earliest times in Hollywood and who still looks spectacular and very attractive.

I look around at the galaxies swirling around me and spy Ginger Rogers at the next table mysteriously melted down like a wax figure but still exuding great warmth and energy to all who come to her table to pay tribute to her. Ah, now Joanie arrives, looking, of course, handmade and resplendent in a Valentino creation, and negotiates her way through the tables like a white water rafter weaving in and out of the rocks, pausing here and there and then swiftly moving on past the little islands of celebrities, her quick hawk's eye scanning the tables for any possible meat, and seeing none worth pausing for, moves swiftly on.

Tony gets up to chat to the audience, thanking them for their support and feeling boosted-up after seeing a quick résumé on the two screens on either side of the stage of his life in motion pictures. He is wearing a trendy black jacket with sleeves made with metal disks giving a kind of armour-plated look that he might have sported in the film *The Vikings*. No shirt but a white low-cut vest and the whole effect topped by a mini-atomic cloud of shocking white hair which our Joan unkindly calls a 'sheital', being Yiddish for an 'Irish' which is slang for a hairpiece, thus betraying her own Jewish origins. The hairpiece, if it is, suits him incredibly well and he looks remarkably preserved. Joan is accompanied by her handsome and multi-talented son Sasha out of Tony Newley. Sasha was a spit of Tony with a touch of Joan's sharpening features.

In these little excerpts which are enthusiastically applauded we see actors who are mummified forever, embalmed in celluloid and eternally young and so the flesh that sits with toupee, watery eyes, bent-over backs are merely the hulk while the 'real' being is out there and as immortal as is the star in the firmament. I feel as if I have entered a private universe by going through the screen into the fourth dimension. The man I ogled as a teenager, the once exotic Tony, is telling us a story. He is joined by his daughter Jamie Lee Curtis who turns out to be an equally splendid and confident raconteur. In my book she could double as a stand-up comedian if she needed a second career. She strides on the stage in a figure-hugging dress that reveals as much leg as possible and confesses she borrowed it from her dad. The house comes down. I recall the Tony Curtis hairstyle that we all loved so much and emulated, pinned up in every barber shop in the country. You chose either a Tony Curtis with a piece flopping over the front of your forehead or a Perry Como which was your cooler, sharp fringe cut and so all these glossy photos stared back at us in three-quarter profile as on Saturday we waited in the barber shops of the world and in my case Stoke Newington.

The rich citizens paid up to $5000 for a seat, the proceeds of which were going to some charity and this allowed them to dart up to our table like hungry old piranhas wanting a bite of the succulent morsel called Joan and begging for a chance to be photographed with her. Some were so desperate, even coming up to her while she was eating and she would firmly but politely tell them to piss off.

The great Donald O'Connor comes back on the stage and winds up the events and recalls Tony Curtis's great success in *Houdini*, commenting that Tony still retains some of those skills since tonight he was able to make two Steak Dianes disappear. For some reason this appeals deeply to my sense of humour and I found an old laugh coming out of me that had been stuck there for some time and now wedged itself loose with an almighty yelp of freedom which drew strange stares from the table as if in pity for my simple-minded British humour. I decide it's time to renew my acquaintance with Tony (we did a pilot for a mini-series six years ago and he was shamefully replaced by George Hamilton). I am hoping that he just might remember me and at the end of the proceedings I swim upstream against the flow of departing guests to where he is still shaking hands, hugging, kissing and being patted. He sees me and in his charming, ineffably sweet way, and why he is so loved, greets me like a long lost friend, throws his arms around me and gives me a big hug and I hug him back. His children are introduced and all claim to have seen my plays! Jamie Lee Curtis actually comes up and introduces herself and suddenly I am in a brace of Curtises. The air is euphoric and a match would ignite it. I say goodbye and as I depart I see Bob Hope slink slowly out and in this case I now become the fan and extend a hand which is firmly taken and Lance manages to get a picture of me and the GREAT BOB.

19
My Film: *Decadence*

Palm Springs

We are destined to meet up at 5.45 p.m. in the lobby and dive into the limo with Joan, her publicist Geoffrey, a smooth billiard ball with a mouth and two eyes that dart sharply atop a gnomish body, Sasha Newley her son and Lance Reynolds. Joan slides in and is firmly ensconced and so I have to make the journey around the front of the limo to the other side whereupon I too slide into the black, velvety hole. Joan, as usual, sounds the first chords upon which we all chime in from time to time as accompanists upon the theme of Joan. Geoffrey is lead violin making continuous pizzicato, Lance comes in as the trombone from time to time while Sasha is an electric guitar sounding some Claptonish riffs and I suppose I play the odd percussion, not a steady thump, but Joan's shrill-like soprano rises over everybody as she goes into the upper octaves.

We slither out after a couple of minutes' driving but since this is not Cannes, LA, London or Venice, we have a moderate bunch of curious spectators outside the movie house and while we are at least a little dressed for the occasion, this bunch look like hillbillies, in jeans, T-shirts and Reeboks. I am slightly aghast but after all this is a casual film festival for offbeat films and this is the first showing of *Decadence*. We all enter with keen anticipation of how Americans will react to this movie which was so thoroughly and disrespectfully trounced in England. I'm still in a semi-comatose state from the jet lag and my mind is a pot-pourri of simmering thoughts as we are gathered at the front of the auditorium, ready to step on stage to say a few words and yet I can't focus without much difficulty and am still in an unreal zone of the senses. Indian nation, Palm Springs, Tony Curtis's party the night before, endless long black, slug-like limos, Joan, hands stretching out from all directions, old memories, but we climb on the stage which is amazingly not lit for the occasion and we are in semi-darkness although the audience is lit and Joan improvises boldly and raps, 'I can see you but you can't see me,' which draws a pon toon of a response and concludes with the usual 'Hope you'll enjoy etc.' and then I am introduced and I still feel like an unknown entity here even with the dozen years I have been coming to both coasts and being welcomed by American generosity and perplexity.

   I recall this cinema over a decade ago when I queued to see *E.T.* here in this old, beautiful, art deco building which feels like a real home for a movie. Next door is one of the best diners in the area called Louis' Pantry, an authentic Norman Rockwell come to life. There was a queue outside the cinema earlier which gladdened my heart until I saw they were queuing for the famous diner! I had scribbled a few notes on the back of a TV menu that I picked up from my hotel and since Lance dared me, I used the occasion of the gloom to say to the audience that I had made some notes but I can't read them now, which earned an unexpected cackle, and then, pretending to read I said, 'Hot dog and french fries, oops sorry!' and another happy cackle swept like a wind across the auditorium. 'This movie house has a special meaning for me since years ago I saw *E.T.* here' and now a fusillade of 'haws' ripped like a sudden squall across the seats and I thought, What on earth was funny about that? I went quickly on to conclude, received a warm clap and sat down in the back row and waited.

I wasn't disappointed and relished the film even more sharing it with 500 new American eyes. The film starts with a mind-boggling, helter-skelter, speeded-up view of London which has everybody reeling. Former 'Police' man Stewart Copeland composed the perfect music for it and now we are into the film and the laughs come fast and frequent as if they are either more tuned in to humour here or they are more eager to vocalise their appreciation since laughter also releases the laugher. The film has never looked so beautiful, shot by French master Denis (*Monsieur Hire*) Lenois. Our producers, thinking it too long, have made some unauthorised cuts and some beautiful elements of slapstick between me and Joan have been surgically removed. Joan is seething two seats away from me and I thought that whoever likes this strange beast of a film will like it whether it has fifteen minutes more or less and whoever hates it will not be seduced by brevity but will hate it even if it was thirty minutes long.

After my first long monologue about the demerits of public school made while eating spaghetti and shot with a locked-off camera there was a spontaneous burst of applause from the audience. I mean how often do you get that? To clap a screen. Unfortunately, however, though it also happened in London, critics didn't see or hear that since they insist, unlike live theatres, in sitting in great cavernous cinemas bereft of audiences. I watch the film unravel as if I had never seen it before. There is a good applause at the end from the packed audience and then we roll out and file into the coffin once again and I begin to feel like a vampire needing my dark home with its black glass windows while outside normal people walk in the daylight.

We now slide off and alight at a smart restaurant where the *hoi polloi* of Palm Springs gather and the room has that excited, slightly hysterical air of the ultra-wealthy being over-stimulated by the presence of other ultra-wealthy. Everybody at our table tries to make a meal out of the experience of the film, picking at this scene and that, turning this one over, discussing its future in America, distribution, compliments, flattery, pain over cuts and eating and ordering which seems to take forever. Joan, meanwhile, is annoyed by the greasy head waiter who every time he comes over puts his hand on her shoulders in that familiar arse-licking gesture of ingratiation. This is so American since they are conditioned by a public who crave and need constant attention and reassurance but the British do not have quite the same anal cravings and find the gesture deeply offensive as does Joan who is getting rattled by his pawing. By now my trousers are cutting into my waist and I can't wait to get back to escape to the sanctuary of my room where like a tubby Superman I burst out of my clothes and repair to Joan's suite where we are all invited for a nightcap. Joan sits cross-legged on the sofa and entertains everybody while we are encouraged to break through our shells and in case we can't she taps on them and makes sure that we do. As I bade my goodnights she was still chatting with great animation. *Sacré bleu!* Where does she get the energy?!

20
Homage to the Hotel du Cap Côte d'Azure

19 June 1995

Perfect breakfast on the terrace: a basket of rolls, croissants perfectly crisp, overblown boomerangs that you anoint with any of the three delicious jars of jam that sit on the table: *miel de France* (honey), *framboise* (raspberry), *Reine Claude* (plum). Each is labelled with a small picture of its contents – a bee, two raspberries, two round green plums – to enable the foreign eyes to identify the succulent fruity pots. A rose plant sits in its terracotta pot on the mottled grey stone table, although it could be marble. Our table is set with rectangles of pink linen upon which are placed our china plates decorated with tiny floral motifs. I pull the tail off a croissant which tears with the expectant resistance of a pastry well baked, unlike their poor British counterparts, those soggy overheated corpses that hang limply like Dali watches. Here the tail gradually yields itself and after its baptism in *Reine Claude* I pour the coffee which comes in a small delicate china pot, that has a leaf motif circling the neck as if it were wearing an emerald necklace and round its body little flowers are scattered. The coffee tastes earthy and brown and brackish and it flows into my vast dry and thirsty gullet while I'm being entertained by the birds' choral orchestra. Sparrows emboldened by the placidity of tourists over the years ignore the sluggish waiter's attempts to shoo them away as they stand on the edge of a bread basket, for all the world as if by long usage it were theirs, and peck away at the Cyclopean rolls that a customer has left behind. Or they stand at a distance and make piercingly sweet requests that you throw them a few crumbs... Meanwhile as the birds cry and tweet, puff their chests out boldly, they advance to the basket of goodies.

On this morning, great rivers of coffee are being poured down the giant throat of France and a million or so croissants are being ripped apart, dipped into coffee, smeared with jam, stuffed with cheese, or grilled with ham. I watch the great mantle of the sea down below our grand white hotel and am able to see the wide shimmering vast Côte d'Azure – azure as the name, as azure as diamonds twinkling, indigo, violet, blue as fields of bluebells, deep aquamarine blue, cornflower blue, deep summer blue. The hot June sun bathes the coastline from Nice to Monaco. St.-Jean Cap Ferrat is a thumb of land sprouting tree-shaded villas, sequestered roads that drowse like it is always Sunday. Avenues of pine, scents of sage, rosemary and lavender fragrantly mix with jasmine, oleander and roses. As you stroll through the odiferous paths, plumes of other activities come sneaking into your alert nostrils as the ladies heat their olive oils and throw in garlic as lunch time signals a whole new waft of smells.

Meanwhile I am still at breakfast and my fruit salad arrives brilliantly festooned in scarlet – bright red raspberries, dissected strawberries, yellow diced guava, amber papayas and orange segments and lightly splashed with the sweetened juice of pears. The birds chirp even more loudly, piercing the air with excitement or naked lust for the food that they see laid out before them. So I tear off a fragment of croissant, which, after a few moments of trembling hesitation, is seized and chewed by a braver fellow, who doesn't even bother to fly away with it since it is not worth the energy, but merely sits on the edge of the table joining me for breakfast.

Now other tables are filling up with the sleepy latecomers enjoying the distinct privilege of opening their eyes on the blissful, wondrous, ethereal sight of a new morning being born out of the moist blue mist. A German family (there are many here) adds another melody with their terrible tongues which sound like people drowning in swamps, scalded snakes or ships' foghorns or a combination of all and they order heavy German breakfasts replete with ham and eggs. I drink the last of the coffee and gaze over the long line of the sea at the edge of the garden and imagine myself in there soon.

I walk up the stairs to our room that overlooks the sky, the leafy treetops and the sea, the tricolour of France through the window. I prepare for the sea and change into trunks, fill a bag with a mask so that I might peer into the mysteries of the depths, grab a camera, towels, books, fruit, lotions, pen, note book and rubber shoes so that I can stand in the water and not suffer a long urchin's spike through my foot.

We go through the garden, past the table where several birds are finishing my uncollected breakfast, through the gate at the end and down the arboreal, well-kept Eden leading to the sea and pool, ignore the pool where the ancient ones are crawling slowly through the overheated, pampered and poisonously chlorinated water, past the limp bodies lying like melted wax reading glossy magazines reporting the inane activities of the world's junk, past the metal gate which takes us out to the small spit of rock from where I sink into the water that surrounds me like a caress. It forms a cool wet embrace round my body and gently licks at my skin with tiny wet kisses and even without peering under the veil of the surface, I can see the small venomous-looking Medusas with their electric trailers hanging from their bodies like tresses. They pulse slowly through the water, a single organism or valve, pumping like a heart. Their shapes are formed by the water and they collapse like a squidge of jelly outside of it, but now, floating in the liquid blue, they resemble starships gliding through space and ready to burn you. So you carefully navigate a passage through them with your eyes open wide beneath the waves, scanning every movement while the ground slowly leaves you. You have then an impression of floating over a huge Venusian landscape, as if you were flying in the land of dreams where without effort you can leave the ground. Often have I flown in my dreams where people stare at you with astonished bewilderment. Now in simulation of this I float weightlessly over the watery abyss, above rocks and crevices, ravines which stretch out into the vast distance all revealed only by a mask which exposes deep gullies, overhangs, and jagged edges of rocky terraces. The waves' giant paws gently try to push you against the rocks and so you must dive and go beneath the turbulence. From below it looks as if the surface was a huge transparent cloth that was being shaken out, a skin, a sheet billowing in the wind, while here all is soft and quiet, yielding, gentle molasses. Striped fish swim in shoals, darting away as you near them and linked in rhythm as if a pack of cards had been thrown in the air and descended in slow motion.

20 June

It is the last day that the croissants come and over the gardens the sea is misty and mercurial blue as the sun washes in from the east. A glorious explosion of swallows whipped past our sleepy room in an early cacophony of squeals, probably chasing swarms of flies. We walk past giant yellow flowers whose vast open trumpets are lined with dark pencil-like streaks, probably landing strips for the bee to hone into before it wriggles itself inside.

Purple bougainvillaea soften the corners of the walls, waiters dance in attendance round the tables in perfect imitation of the bees buzzing round flowers, and the coffee pours again down a million thirsty caverns. The birds cover the gardens with their song, while the sea gently washes against the rocks softened over millions of years, smoothed enough for the thousands of feet that have carefully stepped down into the sea that is as clear as glass and warmed by the sun. As I plunge in I follow a thousand shadows before me and as I sit with my orange juice I occupy a thousand other bodies who have nestled themselves in this wicker chair and happily gazed at the silvery pastel-blue sea with the sky's reflection dotted with speeding swallows. They too opened jars of *Reine Claude* or *myrtille*, while admiring the garden, absorbing the intoxication of smells, the unbottled perfume of lavender, pine and sage. Others too fed morsels to intrepid birds, walked the hot summer Sunday roads of the Cap that lead to rocks, where now they could plunge and float and dream and burn in the sun, and then walked back and heard and tasted and dreamed and woke with the shrilling arpeggios of the swallows and pointed out to each other exotic flowers.

You will cherish the memory and the memory will feed you its moments of the innocent time when all you wanted was a clear sky, the wicker chair, long meandering sun-filled walks... scratched by the briars, clawed by the branches, stung by the mosquitos, chafed by the wind, bruised by the stones, cooled by the sea, astonished by the deep, and soaked by your sweat. After your shower you will look into the mirror and see the day has added its weight to your life until one day you will sink under it, another will sit in your chair and stare and feed the sparrows and open miniature jars of *Reine Claude*.

21
Breakfast at Itala's – Islington

Breakfast, that was always the best time and I can distinctly recall the breakfast my mother used to cook up for me when as an exploding toddler I was terribly partial to fried tomatoes on toast. It was a very piquant taste as I remember and I gulped it down with cups of milky tea and this satisfied me then and ever since. When I left home to fend for myself, I would go round the corner to Itala's little café which sat on the edge of Colbrooke Row in Islington, North London. She greeted me with a large smile which seemed to dissect her face and her son Tony would take my order, which invariably would be an egg on toast with a sausage on the side. She would buzz around her domain chatting and smiling at the customers who were all drawn to the amiable woman and her son until we all became part of her surrogate family.

   She would ask after Annie and then when Annie was no longer with me she was introduced to Shelley and when Shelley and I were no longer together she met Helen and this went on for a short time and she would always ask with a soft and suggestive smile how Shelley was because she liked Shelley. Another day with equal warmth she would inquire after Annie, as if this was her favourite daughter and then another day it would be Helen, and with a slightly different tone for each as if she gauged my feelings and found the apposite note to make the enquiry.

On a sunny day she would put a solitary table outside and then we could pretend to be in the South of France. Sometimes it was scrambled eggs and tomatoes and then there was a time when she grilled cheese on toast for me and that tasted delicious and for a while was my preferred breakfast dish. If it wasn't too busy, I would sit at the corner table and write and occasionally exchange a few words with Tony who was one of those people who knew someone for whatever you needed – minder, electrician, karate teacher, builder, carpenter, etc. – and would sit with me for a while but never too long since he was sensitive to your needs and knew when the air was getting tight around us. Then the odd local would come in, like the writer who lived round the corner and wrote a screenplay called *Throb* and continuously asked me to read *Diary of a Hero* by Lermon tov. There were sunny days and I'd get up, feed the cat and really look forward to my breakfast in Itala's. I knew it would generally be tasty until one day she got rid of the grill for some unknown reason and I could no longer have my melted cheese on toast, heightened sometimes by a slice of lean ham on it. I was most disappointed.

In a lull, Itala would speak of vast changes she hoped to make to create the perfect environment for this little charming front room and every few years her fantasies would be fulfilled and she'd look at you eagerly for approval; once an effect of stained glass windows, another time, a complete change of furniture. I first discovered this café when rehearsing Macbeth in a church hall in Devonia Road and went in there for some take-away teas. She had just moved in and the tables were (charmingly!) sewing-machine bases but these were soon got rid of. Years later she bought a small dog which still barks ferociously for its size and seems to have a mean temper.

When I moved back to the East End, I visited her less and

less but on occasion, I'd go and say hello to Tony and ask if he's getting married to that girl he's courted for over ten years and now he has and has made the final move away from Mum, I imagine. I recall all the customers who became part of her family, the showroom designers from next door who became friends just because we met in Itala's. One of them looked me up when I was directing *Agamemnon* in Israel and he was charming, funny and very gay and very sadly the last I heard of him was that he was dead. I must go back there, since I visited her café for over fifteen years! Unbelievable. I had more breakfasts with her than with my own mother but in a way she was a kind of universal mother and when in one of my unhappy, romantic states she would accommodate her thoughts to suit my mood and reflect. 'That woman wasn't for you,' and 'The other one was much nicer.' She saw and sees everything and the last woman I brought in also said hello but she didn't like to go out for breakfast as much as I did.

I'd go out, buy the *Guardian* and then I'd enjoy reading it from cover to cover and linger over breakfast if I wasn't working and I had nothing else to do. I desperately wanted to be a Shakespearean actor and did audition after audition for the Halls and Nunns and whoever else stood in for them but got nowhere. Now I am a director and direct my own plays including Shakespeare and I am still foolish enough to ask for a space to bring my work but still curiously enough get nowhere and so never learn. Build your own church. But it was in Islington that I started to be independent in the church hall where we rehearsed each evening from 5 p.m. until ten. I would sit with my assistant Chris Munke, a highly intelligent young American, and we would drink Itala's teas and eat her toast and the conducivity of the atmosphere led us always to some good solutions. I was sorry to lose Chris, who eventually drifted into the outer regions. But Itala was always there for me and for us, for words of cheer and words of comfort, for concern and curiosity. I want to go back there now even as I write this and I know she will say, 'And how is that woman who went to America and used to sing?' They often talked of opening in the evening as a bistro; this was a small fantasy which fuelled many a debate and one day I do believe they tried it, but it did not work out so well since Itala's was really an upmarket Italian greasy spoon café, which is not to diminish it, since that kind of working-class to middle-class food was the best you could get.

22

Ha! Ha!

'I have a spare ticket for Glyndebourne,' said my friend, 'and I know you have never been there.' I leapt at the chance since it is a turning off the A22 that I have never taken but which beckoned as I passed it frequently on the way to Brighton where we have a sanctuary overlooking the corrugated waves of the Channel. It seemed a turn off to a place that was never meant for me, a private cultural club set in the rolling, spinach-green hills of Sussex. So without much ado I entered the narrow road that led me to the great House of Opera.

Once at Victoria Station on a sunny day I saw my former-publisher John Calder buying tickets and looking strange in a dinner jacket at two in the afternoon. I retained the image of summer heat and an incongruously dressed man puffing at the ticket booth while clutching a picnic basket. It was, so to speak, '*à rebours*' or against the grain.

I nosed my old silver 4.2 Jag confidently into the wild copses and thickets of undulating Sussex and followed the other cars of the same species that were happily wending their way to what might have been a clan gathering in black and white. Ah, there's the entrance. I pull the old girl over to the left, bumping gently over the sleeping policemen as have the others before me until we all resemble a kind of conga of Jags dancing our way to the immense car park. A kindly attendant waves us happily on to where there are spaces in this immense stretch of hill which rises a few more feet before dropping over the horizon on which delicately shaded cows are contentedly munching.

I park my car amongst hundreds of others all disgorging their cheerful human occupants, no less happy than the cows, and clutching hampers of all sizes, baskets, fold-up chairs and tables, wine coolers, blankets, a whole panoply of paraphernalia. Like refugees on the march, except for wearing the mandatory penguin suits (some had white jackets, much more elegant), they made their way down the hill to what seemed an endless variety of entrances. To my horror I saw that I had committed the gravest error and was the only man in sight not wearing black tie! Ye gods, I had worn a very elegant cut-off jacket like a kind of bolero number that grazed your hips, some shiny narrow pants I had bought in Nice and some semi-Cuban heels but with a BLACK SHIRT! I felt totally out of sync as I watched the bland languid miens trotting down the hill ALL dressed in the correct uniform and I had already sartorially registered my outsider status, my alien qualifications.

Erroneously and because the opera started as it usually does at 4 p.m. I had the idea of matinée in my mind. Now, I was meeting my friend at a place she had called the Ha-Ha. Since my friend had a strong South-American accent I deduced that she was saying 'garden' with much salsa in the voice. She had asked me to bring a rug and so I gathered a nice warm tartan rug from the car and didn't quite feel so horribly out of place as I too had things to gather up and look happily 'busy' and not like a criminal on the run who still had his prison shirt on. So I followed the happy stream down to the garden passing a large hall filled with tables several of which already had hampers and cutlery set out for the interval and so, trying to second-guess,

I laid my tartan blanket (which used to be my late cat's rug) on an available table along with a bottle of champagne I had swiftly bought on the way down just ten seconds before the off-licence closed, since my friend requested a small contribution. At least I had THAT!

Now I drifted along what seemed at times like a maze, a lawned area protected by large hedges and where already some opera lovers were sipping their chilled champagne and trying to keep the nip out of the wind by clinging to the wall of green. At last I espied Estella and her two elegant German friends and we greeted with all that slightly overheated formality that people of culture tend to have as if they hadn't seen each other for a dozen years. I met her German colleague, a banker, who had on his penguin suit which accorded nicely with his silver lank hair. We made our way to the building where the warning bells were sounding for the commencement of the opera.

I forgot to mention that I actually (and feeling rather silly) asked an attendant to name possible meeting places because each area had its name as the place was far to large to simply say, 'See you in front of the theatre.' I couldn't bring myself to say the words 'Ha-Ha' since I was convinced that I had misheard her and Lo and behold! as the attendant kindly rattled off the various normal appellatives she really did utter the words Ha-Ha! Oh how refreshingly cute that there is such a name and I had not even flinched when Estella said, obviously with some degree of relish like tasting a familiar and yet slightly exotic dish, 'See you by the Ha-Ha.' I should have responded with 'What the fuck's that?' or 'Excuse me, darling, would you mind repeating that?' but I didn't and possibly she felt a tad let down since she then could have had the insider's joy of explaining it. I responded as if I go to Glyndebourne once a week and the 'Ha-Ha' was our usual meeting spot, darling.

Now we were there I felt better, more at one with the world, a temporary member of the Ha-Ha's and Lo and behold! there lay a hamper on the ground with glasses and a champagne cooler and as we chattered nobody even mentioned my black shirt but I, yes I, had to confess my abject guilt and horror at my solecism and almost pleaded for redemption from the elegant banker from Germany who shamed me with his perfect English compared to my slovenly German and his coiffed silver hair and knowledge of all the operas. 'Ach no, you look perfectly elegant and after all you are an *artist*,' he responded with the perfect affability and diplomacy you might expect from one with silver hair who wore the correct outfit for Glyndebourne and takes fellow bankers to Wimbledon.

I stared out at the munching cows serenely gazing up from time to time at what for them must be as pleasant as it is for us gazing at them. The black and white seated figures chomping away at their foie gras and salmon sandies must reassure the cows that all is eternal and that nothing will ever spoil nor change this bucolic scene. Each summer they (the humans) will come back and the cows may get a crust of brown bread thrown their way or even a chewy corner of a croissant that had proved too tough for a dentally-challenged visitor. But as I watched this animated Constable setting I no longer felt so estranged but now truly part of the lawn, the countryside, the middle-class cows, Sussex, my friends and the Ha-Ha. But now we were to enter the beautifully new carpentered auditorium which was built in a frenzy or symphony of light wood, as if a carpenters' consortium had got together and decided to make a barn that looked like a theatre.

We were watching *Eugene Onegin* by Tchaikovsky, a moving and haunting melodrama of lost love and bitter disappointment. The lights went down on the plush audience and even went down on my black shirt and so now I was enveloped in the velvety blackness of white, elegant, upper class, distingué England and I settled back. The white curtains that veiled the set were ever so delicately draped slightly to one side as if even they might be the very same drapes that hang in the bedrooms of the audience and I could almost hear the thoughts of women approving the gathering of the folds and making mental notes to reproduce this effect at home. The curtains unfolded to reveal an oatmeal-coloured set and a shaved cornfield which somehow harmonised with the interior of the theatre. We were awash in browns and beige, wheat colours and homespun; it almost might be an ad for Hovis, the kind you used to see in the Underground.

The singers started and we saw the gentle beginnings of the peasant girl in her sweet little bed falling in love with her dashing beau and the music swelled and rolled into our ears from time to time, the shades of darkness slipped over my brain and I fell into a split-second twilight world where snatches of dreams wilfully tormented me but then I'd recover and try to concentrate on the agonies of unrequited love.

The first interval, some Pimms and off to Act II with more vigour and semi-wildish balls, pirouetting dancers, the music rises, a duel, a death and I stayed completely awake this time. Now the second interval and the famous picnic break and the reason why we are all here, since the opera is only one part of the grand *esprit de corps*. For now we are to partake of our picnic, even if some have nibbled already. We dine alfresco and like busy little bees we set the blanket, put down the plates, open the champers, nosh the deli, chew the chicken and surrounding us on collapsing tables, or on blankets like us, or little stools, the audience were chuckling, nibbling, pouring, giggling, opening their carefully prepared packets, plastic containers, hampers with Harrods printed on the outside, juices, coffee flasks, pâtés and caviar. We too were part of the medley and even I, sitting there gazing at the hills undulating away into the distance, was part of it and I thought of all those busy fingers who did it themselves, the morning's preparation, the shopping in Fulham the day before, the anticipation, the planning like an assault by an armed force, the filling of the car, the tickets, the food, the event! At the end – Tchaikovsky!

Men passed by giving me the odd look of disdain and when

I was looking for Estella I recalled feeling so much like an outsider in my black shirt and Cuban-heels that I had hoped the audience might mistake me for an attendant or a steward of some kind. Now I am sipping the magic plonk, eyeballing the cows that are coming ever closer but are prevented from invading by a ditch. 'Oh, look at this view,' my companions exclaim as if to make sure that we are all in a suitable state of awe and exultation to be here and enjoying our £75 seats. We all murmur with cooing satisfaction although there is a wind chill factor that is creeping upon us and crawling into our bones, although my companion hostess had an indomitable spirit that nothing can bend as we continue to slug back the champers even though we still have an act to go.

'Yes, let's get a coffee,' my German friend suggests, to get warmed up and we approach the bar at which one solitary plump girl waddles around grinning, not unlike the happy expression of the cows, and appears to ignore us. The bar is loaded with used coffee cups which appears to be normal since she makes no attempt to clear them up even after she serves us. Perhaps they're all volunteers. But now the chill plus filled bladders, has everyone travelling downstairs to go to the loo and for the first time in my life I can understand why Orthodox Jews thank God for the gift of maleness over femaleness. I had never seen such a queue for the women's loo in my life. It stretched across the whole foyer as they stood docilely like cows about to be slaughtered with ne'er a whimper when it would have been just as easy to take a leak in the grassy fields. In fact why not set up some portakabins discreetly disguised, perhaps with rippling curtains. The men's urinals were of course packed and the sight of a group of men dressed in identical black facing a wall was the most fascinating sight I had seen in years. The frenzy now to rid oneself of all this liquid was beginning to corrode the aesthetic nature of the event for at this moment the downstairs area felt like an Australian cattle station on market day.

Eugene Onegin was definitely taking second place to a good slash and as I left the men's room the women's queue was now longer than ever and indeed it looked like Macbeth's vision when he sees his opposition's descendants: 'What, will the line stretch out to the crack of doom.' I took my seat for the final act and presumed that somehow the women made their way back or are still there. The curtains waved back and forth revealing new scenes and the heroine sang bravely and beautifully and there were some rather militant 'Bravos' every time someone sang with some emotion but as I looked into the audience I knew that everyone had just been to the loo and because I had seen them standing facing the wall all dressed in black and looking soppy they didn't seem such a special club anymore but more like a lot of kids on a picnic and having a bit of entertainment on the side. It was a beautiful if underpowered opera and we all poured out making those apposite comments that one is supposed to make.

We parted and I drove to my little escape in Brighton and as I steered the old lady across the downs I saw one of the most beautiful sunsets I had ever witnessed in my life. So it was all very worthwhile, if you can afford it of course.

23

Christmas in the Caribbean

Went for a long walk in the morning to the local town of Soufrière, which means sulphur since it is located near the sulphur spring that was used in French colonial times. The soldiers took advantage of its healing properties to treat their aliments. Now the tourists bathe in it. The town was quiet. A poor black tries to panhandle from me and asks if I am Santa. Yes, of course, I vaguely reply. Then quick as a whippet he retorts, 'Then where is my present?' He wears a pair of grubby shorts and is as poor as Death. His hair is long and matted and he could be a lapsed Rasta and one who aspires to spend his life stoned. The town rots in poverty and cheapness and at night it tries to come to life with little stalls cooking up some shreds of meat. The French colonial square sits attractively in the middle of the town as a meeting and breathing place but now it's a dead square where a few Rastas hang about playing the incessant same music and folk sit clumped closely together on the wall or in the shadows of doorways. Perhaps they hope that something will happen – Bob Marley has given them some branch to hold on to but it is not enough to nourish all their needs. They sit quietly as if robbed of that which would give their lives colour or definition... always hanging around and endless jump-ups which are joyful occasions to let off some steam and then it's back to the hanging around.

Drove to Choisil, a little fishing village, a few shabby stalls in the street, some old hags are eating some scrawny chicken at the outdoor stove. One of them generously throws a thin chicken bone she has sucked clean to a dog who walks on three legs while holding up his wounded paw to which nobody pays the slightest attention. It swiftly goes to retrieve the meatless bone. Leaning against some fishing boats are the town's local boys, a few lithe muscled blacks, their abdominal muscles worn as a kind of corrugated badge that reveals their occupations as manual, hard, worthy and demanding, probably pulling in the nets. Most blacks share this muscled 'shield' of flesh which contrasts to the white tourists' flaccid bellies, their loose carpets of lard. The women like to sit on steps by their houses surrounded by their brood and keep producing and so it goes on with good humour, eating, drinking, jump-ups, fishing, hanging out, waiting, and putting curlers in their hair and breeding. The men mostly stay around the square, waiting, simpering, raging within. Hard faces watching us as we pass by, just eyes moving while the face remains still.

Spreading out from the town on either side are roads that may as well lead to the town of Oz for all the effect it will have on them. These roads are inaccessible to most of them for they lead to paradise, civilisation, resorts where the white soft-bellied cream of Europe and America stay. These are small utopias dedicated to easing the anguish of mercantile life and wintry drabness with the promise of sunny island charm and the natives' white-toothed smiles serving you breakfast on balconies. Here in this tiny enclave of luxury, well protected by the ever-watchful eye of security, the white man can stretch out in rooms of unimaginable splendour, huge high, airy, wooded rooms with ravishing views over the cobalt-blue sea and emerald forests and sleep peaceably between freshly laundered cotton sheets as delicate as silk. Dinner is served by well-trained, warm-hearted black mamas with cute bandanas in their hair and freshly laundered gingham-check uniforms. The mamas enquire, as they have been programmed to, each night about your day as if it was the sole source of their joy whether you had a pleasant afternoon of snorkelling, swimming, diving or even just sunbathing with a junk book. So 'How was your day?' is the refrain from smiling white teeth, beautiful skin and hand-picked from the village of sulphur where the less fortunate sit in doorways and watch. They seem happy to have a job here. After they finish a reasonable shift of eight hours, a small bus collects them and after checking in their handbags, the driver returns them to their village along the horribly broken road which is left bumpy and potholed apparently to deter vehicles to casually visit. The natives of course would not be necessarily welcome in the bars.

Last evening a black singer of unimaginable sweetness sang to a group of yacking Christmas Eve idiots who were so involved in telling their stories of mind-wrenching banality detailing how pissed they got the night before and how long it took to sober up. The singer didn't even have a spotlight to pick him out so you were unable to make out more than a blob of darkness where his face should be, but you imagined from the impeccable delivery of his bluesy tones another Marvin Gaye. One could with pleasure listen to this Orpheus all night as he charms the stones and makes the stars stand still and listen. A native comes round incongruously dressed as Santa. A woman tourist drunkenly shrieks, 'WHATCHA GOT FOR US, SANTA?!!'

The stars bulge in the heavens as if they were overripe fruit waiting to be picked... the little goats munch contentedly by the roadside ignoring the cars and jeeps that narrowly miss them and blissfully unaware that on this Christmas Eve their minutes are ticking away since this is the festive time of the great meaty feasts on the island.

Now, on the other side of Soufrière is a long winding road

that snakes its way out of the stew of human existence, out of that melting pot and climbs gratefully into the fresh, sweet, clean air. As you leave Soufrière, since you cannot bypass it, the last few stragglers call out to you in hope that in exchange for some info like 'Waterfall?' or 'Sulphur baths?' you may donate a dollar or two. On the left over the bridge you pass the big rubbish tip filled to overflowing and swiftly ascend into Paradise once more. The road rises, gradually reducing the horrors of Soufrière to a pleasant picture postcard and you are unable to smell the intolerable stench of the shanty town on the beach or see the junk thrown into the river even if a notice forbids it.

Once free of the poor town we make a turn and head to the other paradise called the Jalousie Plantation founded originally by Lord Glenconner who now owns only a small portion of it. The resort is set in the most beautiful valley on the entire island and situated between two gigantic and mysterious hills perfectly formed into cones called the Pitons which shelter the beautifully tailored tourist village. It's dotted with little cottages each with its mini plunge pool for those too tired to jump on to a passing courtesy bus that would deposit them on the shore. There are rolling lawns, tennis courts, swimming pools and a beach that stretches itself out between the two peaks and at the end is the 'Lord's' plantation house which resembles nothing less than a set from *Porgy and Bess*. You expect that at any moment a window will fly open and a black servant will sing, 'Bess, you is mah woman now'. There is a kind of simple pirate's bar at the side serving your rum punches and in the middle of the courtyard an open area which has a stage in the centre. The Lord Glenconner can be seen wandering through his reduced estate dressed completely in white like a ghost of something past, a wraith in a large white hat, flowing white shirt and white trousers. He perambulates the grounds putting one in mind of some distressed spirit that cannot rest and is tormented by some hideous event.

The Jalousie beach is perfectly situated to be able to watch the sun sinking into the centre of the sea like an egg yolk diving into a frying pan. You can have lunch at the beachside restaurant and so earlier we shared a salad. There are many Americans here and opposite a little spoilt girl is delivered a hot dog in a large dry roll. She plays with her food like many Yankee children do who are overfed and must obey ritual hours to be told when they are hungry. Although the buffet is full of salads and fruit, she picks lazily at her revolting dog. We are visitors to Jalousie and a pale skin eases your entrance and the barrier goes up and then you park your car and wait for the shuttle. Some guests seem to have been issued with their own electric cars which they putter around in and over the perfect roads and manicured lawns, and I am reminded of a strange TV series starring Patrick McGoohan called *The Prisoner* where a man is kept incarcerated in a strangely bland Utopia.

After a glorious swim in the silky blue sea by a coral reef at the edge of the Pitons and studying the most incredible variety of sea life known to man, we wander over to the edge of the estate where Lord Glenconner has his tiny empire and where we can watch the sun slowly be sucked into the belly of the sea. We enter a gate into a strange kind of compound which we took at first to be the staff quarters and I had even mentally congratulated the Lord for making a place just for the staff but this was for us, the tourists. It's called Bangs and I'm reminded of how the British aristos love the feeling of something slightly rundown. A few cushioned benches line the beach and it's all a bit 'raffish' and a bit worn out... and charming, of course. I order a punch and it tastes like liquid sunset and as I sip the chilled nectar through a straw I espy the Lord stalking his estate like a wandering Jew, as if cursed never to be able to rest. He is the perfect paradigm of shrunk colonialism as he circles then goes out of sight behind the house and then reappears again, stopping only to give occasional and probably unnecessary orders to his staff. His wide-brimmed hat sits atop a tall imposing and handsome figure, a touch of Don Quixote. As the sun is setting a few tables are collecting their evening guests and now my Lord appears again like a Caribbean Roderick Usher but this time he stops at a table and chats to the guests who are visiting his 'Empire', impressing the visitors with his regal presence, his cane, white fedora, and whistle round his neck which, I guessed, was to enable him to call his staff from wherever he has wandered. Eventually he comes to us since we look up expectantly hoping to be blessed by his presence. My built-in conditioned reflex almost impels me to kneel but before I can he has taken a seat and charmed us with his personality, putting us lesser mortals at ease in the ineffable way that aristos have.

Then not wishing to exhaust us by us having to be on high alert for His Majesty he chose to leave as our fish cakes arrived which are a speciality of the Caribbean and these are the very best I have eaten on this island. Now the main fish turns up in a Creole sauce, a small hill of plantains and dasheen. It tastes sublimely good as food does in the open air. The band plays the same songs as it has run through its repertoire in thirty minutes and the stars have grown somewhat larger as if they too have been feeding. The rum punch courses its way through the avenues of the body like a snake has been let loose and now the head starts to move to the music and then the feet and then the diaphragm all independent of each other. The Lord has made a splendid environment and he looks well pleased with his domain. We return leaving the huge controlled environment of Jalousie full of Americans and their awful children, descend the hill and once more are in the sleepy village of Soufrière. A few dark faces still sit in the darkened streets and they will never know or see what goes on only a couple of miles from them and it may as well be on the moon. Over the scarred and broken road we bump until we arrive at the other sanctuary of beautiful Anse Chastanet. The tree frogs are making the most beautiful music and will lull us into a blissful sleep. And so we bounced from one paradise at Jalousie between the Pitons to the other on the far side of the green cones. It is like we are trapeze artists swinging on a pendulum, careful to avoid falling into the middle into the town of Sulphur where the people wait... silently and patiently.

24
Bondi

In Ozzyland a day in Bondi Beach is first of all covered with a faint pale blue sky that stretches across the window of your hotel room, filling it completely. A perfect square of blue becomes a magic carpet that you leap on to take yourself down to Bondi Beach which has been the Mecca for the Aussies from time immemorial and whether in Gallipoli, dying like flies on the notorious Burmese railway during World War II or rotting in a damp Earls Court bedsitter, an Ozzy's mind will take comfort from letting it drift towards Bondi.

Bondi is a small suburb of Sydney possessing a long wide scalloped beach about a mile long, a curved arena fringed with small hotels and cafés that sit staring out on to the deep blue waters of the Pacific. Bondi encircles its beach like a protective arm cradling its young and old. You go there when a stripling – bouncing on your surfboard like a little sea god and it will record your journey into old age as you sit crustily chewing your memories, squinting into the perfect sunset. If you feel like walking there is a breathtaking winding path to the next beach of Tamorama, the kind of walk that imprints itself on your mind forever and the Ozzy child will take it for granted since it is just a suburb of Sydney that you will only think of affectionately when thousands of miles away from it.

The hedonistic Sydneyite explodes on to the beach on weekends and celebrates his sense of well-being in a way that the poor Brits, chained to the habits that sadistic weather has ingrained in them, can never quite achieve on the stony beaches of Brighton or the sleazy sand dunes of Southend. For the Brits, sun tends to cause confusion, agonies of decision, giant traffic jams and murderous tensions.

In Bondi the beach is innocent and taken for granted. It is the gym, the meeting place, the sexual zone, the sanctuary and the playground. You can try any of the hundred cafés lining the beach, eating a well stuffed foccaccia (the Ozzy's favourite Italian sandwich) while watching the gladiators of the surf riding their foaming horses like rodeo riders. They float, bobbing on the waves seagull-like, waiting until the big one sneaks up on them. Then gripping their boards, they manage to stand on them balancing themselves and defying the thousand ripples of the sea-monster's muscles flexing its back to try and shake them off.

Meanwhile on the pathways other young gladiators are strengthening their limbs as they cut through the morning air on their rollerblades. Rollerblades revolutionised the four-wheel skate as did the two-wheeler the old three-wheel bike. At the edge of the beach there is a pit where the young tyros perform stomach-churning acrobatic feats diving down a sharply inclined ramp and such is the velocity that they are scooped up the other side where, for a second, escaping gravity, they hang weightless in mid-air and then repeat the process tearing down the mini ski-slope. If unusually intrepid they will, at the weightless moment, perform a somersault and go down backwards. After the event the tiny glads sit on a ramp and await their next turn. Helmeted miniature future astronauts surveying their terrain. None of them is over fourteen and some look eight or nine!

The rest of us are contented just to strap our futuristic rollerblades on and gently slide down the boardwalk to the Pavilion and sit and drink endless cappuccinos surrounded by the ubiquitous Japs buzzing around taking pictures. The Japs really like Ozzyland, some so much that they are buying most of it up. Of course there is always the café where the 'faces' hang out and that's at the edge of the beach, the far end away from tourists where you sit outside at large well-worn wooden tables, order flat whites, eat huge greasy-spoon breakfasts and greet your mates from the city as you progress along from one café to another. But for now you watch the triple flag of sky, sea and sand, it is the familiar flag of life. It nourishes, gladdens the eye and supports the spirit.

The narrow streets off the prom are small-town affairs with boutiques and bookshops. There are lots of bookshops in Sydney and I drift in always on the look-out for my plays. I see that an old play of mine, *East*, is advertised as being on in the Bondi Pavilion, so I stroll along to this kind of community centre where they have exhibits and performances but *East* has performed its last on the previous Saturday – so I'm now part of the Ozzy culture. I sit and imbibe yet another coffee outside the Pavilion and watch the kids tumbling out of the buses with their little surfboards, keen to dance upon the ever-obliging waves and take their Bondi for granted and, as I sit, I am grateful to my work that transports me to other lands on a magic carpet.

25

Leaving Oz:
In memory of Brian Hagland

Monday, 11 November

This will be my last day in Oz and I decide to go to Bronte in this beautiful early morning and sit in the sun while staring at the sea. I had made arrangements to see Robert MacFarlane and so I get there early and gaze at the silent waves (since I am far off) pouring beautifully, dutifully, gracefully, copiously, splendidly and colourfully in. My heart has been heavy at the thought of leaving and even overflowed, pouring its own tides down the hills of my cheeks. The waves are faintly sibilant and amethyst blue with touches of green jade further out. The sky is a perfect cornflower blue. It was a chilly morning when I took off from my hotel at 7.30 a.m. and while the vision was summer, the feel was early spring and I regretted not bringing a jacket as I sped in my open-top convertible through King's Cross heading down to Edgecliff and then on to Bondi, taking my favourite route which gives the wide expanse of Rose Bay and the view of the majestic Sydney skyline. Head right for Bronte and then wind your way down sniffing for the sea. How limited time concentrates the mind like an execution when every moment is the most precious in life and so today I have divided the time among my nearest and dearest; each hour a small piece of eternity.

I arrived and parked, walked down the hill where the Sea-Juiced Café had just opened for the day which I could only be a small part of but was grateful for, so much so that I took my own table outside since they hadn't been set yet. There was just one early couple outside since the café fills quickly with those eager to drink the juice of the earth while watching the movement of the ever-thrashing wild and wondrous surf. I watched the silent waves swamp the shore in salty wet kisses. Then appearing as if out of my past was Ralph Cotterill. He walked like an old actor with a cane and is a youthful sixty-five. We were both pleased to see each other and greeted like long-lost friends. I had half expected to see him since I had heard from a mutual acquaintance that he rises early and like a Galapagos Island lizard suns himself by the pool. His eyes were bright blue as if his genes had his sea-faring ancestors' eyes in them and his head was full of Bronte sunsets and seascapes and he proceeded to tell me his story.

The ancient mariner told me of exotic lands, Burma, strange islands, the class he is doing in Chinese so as to be able to converse with his new friend in Thailand. He told me about the move from Lang Road opposite Centennial Park (which I have marked with my sweat three times a week skating along its paths and which I have grown to love) and the view he has from Bronte where he lives above the cemetery where many famous people have chosen to be buried. The table was still in the shade as the sun had not yet turned the corner but was a few feet away from me and I felt chilled, so I stretched out my hand to where I felt the soft warm on it and gathered up a cupful. Ralph ordered café latte, toast and jam. Curiously that morning he was doing a radio programme on Van Gogh, a character he even resembles since like Vincent, Ralph has his mystery. He looks like a buccaneer, a pirate, part-time clown, rustic, rural imp, philosopher, actor. Yes, you can be all these things but sometimes you want it for real.

Just then as I was listening to Ralph while admiring the cobalt-blue sky and apple-green sea comes the Falstaffian girth of photographer Robert MacFarlane, an old memory also from the magic year of '78. I like an ally who is as a brother or a cousin and with these two friends, no matter what years come between us, there is a sense of continuity when we meet up again. Ralph was my insect man in *Metamorphosis* and Robert was the photographic recorder of at least four of my shows. And they are both people I might have missed seeing but for the last day's concentration of the mind which perforce demands that I regard all that's special to me in the land of Oz. I feel Robert's girth against me as he hugs me like some huge dolphin and yet he looks Buddhist and benign, swimming calmly in his life as in his copious layers of wobble. He carries no grief within him although he lost his son in a street accident and endures the agony of the remaining son who is handicapped. In Robert's case, would I be insufferably romantic to say he uses suffering to sweeten him? His wife has just up and departed although he is not sure whether this is good or bad. I now hesitate to ask when I see how things are, lest the news is mournful but now he pulls up a chair and basks in the sunshine. He gives me a present – a diary accompanied by many of his photos, in which I am included playing Roderick Usher (or in my version anyway) as a human being on the extreme verge of disintegration. Ralph beams and Robert curiously mentions his extraordinary blue eyes which I have already remarked on once this morning, for it seems as if Ralph has a portion of the sea in them hence he is always drawn to come back to it each day.

We were all united in the Nimrod Theatre (as it was then

called) production of the Kafka play as director, performer and recorder. So we are buried like archaeological artefacts in the substratum of human memory. We are no more than shards occasionally dug up by some magazine or periodical making some point about the theatre in '78 but for us the year is still quivering in our unconscious and draws us to be together again in a seance for that blissful sunny time. We must not fade away in old programmes and curling posters in some forgotten cupboard. We are missing Nik Lyons who created such a memorable tapestry of music to clothe the play in. Two years ago a thin, gaunt chap came up to me after I had finished my one-man-show one night at the Athenaeum Theatre Melbourne, and said, 'I'm Nik Lyons. Don't you remember?' I remembered him with flaring, thick, shoulder-length blonde hair, laughing blue eyes like Ralph and a strong virile body, able even to climb up the scaffolding set like a young kid. Lack of work had driven him away from the society that no longer nourished him and like many others he had fled into the non-judgemental 'Bush' – the expression used here for the Outlands. I saw him in the foyer posing as a down-and-out or maybe this is how one looks when away from the vanities of society. I remember seeing George Shvetsov who played the father in *Metamorphosis* when I was playing *Salome* in Perth four years ago and wondering what on Earth had happened to him. Again thin, gaunt, somewhat shabby and unkempt but full of life and now he's actually starring in a film called *Love Serenade* and doing very well.

By now the three of us resembled three old pigeons waiting for the sun to come out and warm our wings. Robert, a boxing fan, talked about the big fight between Tyson and Holyfield. He enthused and discussed most eloquently and knowledgeably the finer points, helping me to make up for what I had so stupidly missed. Bob offered to loan me his taped copy but today of all days left me no time for the simple sweetmeats of life. As he spoke, I could see the wide blue sea moving under the sea urchins that waited on the waves to be pushed up and sent slithering down. Robert goes through the itinerary of courage, power and daring that was exhibited that night and I see that he must like to watch acts of grit and stamina and is drawn to such people who display it. He also captures an essence in his shots and I recall when I first met him while playing in *East* at the suitably named Walhalla in Glebe Point Road. He sat in the circle and while seeing the show for the first time was also able to shoot the best pictures of that play I have ever had. They were shot live and the difference between live and rehearsed is immense since before the live audience you are prepared as for combat and, whatever you are feeling, have to be brave.

So Bob talked of men and women he had observed going through the birth pangs of creation: the wonderful Valery Panov, the Russian dancer who like Baryshnikov leapt to freedom, but unlike Mischa never found fame since he was already in his thirties and could not be for the public a Russian fawn who had wandered into their garden. Panov was lithe, dark, saturnine and too Semitic to enchant the West, but I did see Panov dance Petruschka in London when he was quite brilliant and a born clown. Panov spent some time in Oz, where Bob photographed him. Then he told me a funny story about meeting Henry Cooper, our last real heavyweight who dines out on the story of how he gave Ali the punch that nearly put him out. According to Bob or Cooper, Ali's glove was split and it was claimed the trainer ripped it to allow more time for Ali to recover. When Cooper made Ali's knees wobble he opened the door to immortality by just a chink but in the next round Ali slammed it shut in his face.

So in the sun on Bronte we exchanged a kind of fevered frisson that you might extend to a man who has not got much time on this Earth, which I hadn't. We were three planets in almost perfect alignment and who knows when this configuration would happen again? The great German actor

Eckhard Schall then entered our stream of chat since Bertold Brecht's son-in-law had actually played his one-man show in the Nimrod Theatre of all places. Bob's photograph of him shows an intense man clutching himself round the shoulders while dressed in a well-tailored, striped, double-breasted suit and how powerful he looks as he rehearses his act. Of course I have a very strong memory stored away of Schall playing in *Arturo Ui* at the National Theatre in the days when they invited great artists to visit. Those were Olivier's days and Ken Tynan's.

Robert ordered toast and latte and the café was now filling up with chatty breakfasters while we kept telling stories as if to weave around each other a psychic skein, something to spiritually bind us together in memory until we fill those spaces again. Just then Zelda walks past, mermaid-like, since she has just had her early morning swim and her hair was twisted into salty braids. She had swum in the small, open-air pool that abuts the sea and is fed by it and is a piece of the sea which is trapped and tamed enough for the old codgers and kids to swim in. So after we parted, Ralph, Robert and I, the temptation of a swim lured me to the pool which in true Ozzie spirit is free, just like it might be a park and it is built in such a way that it seems to need little maintenance. I left my clothes on a bench and for a while sat there letting the sun do its stuff and delighting in its caresses and it felt precious and rare since it was only going to be there for me a few moments more. The time graciously stopped for a while and I watched the bobbing surfers waiting patiently for the big one, the way an actor waits for the phone to ring. It may not but you somehow expect that it will. I decided to plunge in and it was much colder than I had imagined it would be. I felt the chill eating right into me and I skewed through the water and rushed out into the sun again. The old guys were doing their regular, chilly laps while I looked on in admiration for their hardiness.

My heart was heavy since I couldn't believe how I could leave this friendly city with the crashing blue waves splintering on the yellow sands under a washed blue sky. Above me on the next level, old codgers whose habits have probably taken them here for years chatter seagull-like about the Tyson fight. A younger man banters with an old man whose shanks seem to be weathered and cured by the sun like old leather and whose arms still bore the faint blue graffiti of his youth tattooed with 'Mum' and such-like other holy objects of his life. My body felt cleansed after my last baptism and I drove away from Bronte.

Reaching my hotel, I deposited my convertible for the last time and continued the sad collecting of my two-month life in that hotel room. The hundreds of photographs neatly arranged in a large book bought from 'Quickiephotos' in the Cross. The new books including Robert Drew's *Drowning* given to me as a first night gift by John (*Coriolanus*) Bell and an old Plutarch *Life of the Romans* so that I could read about this man I have been analysing and staging for the last five or six years. I bought that in a lovely old book shop in Oxford Street. The unputdownable *Sex, Love and Death* which deals with the unbearable preciousness of life when the sentence of Aids is upon you. For some, Aids, while being a curse, was a revelation of how one had squandered the precious staff of life. I have to call the writer Margaret Gee who sent me a charming essay on Byron Bay that had been commissioned by some magazine or other and she sent it since she spied me one morning sitting alone at the breakfast table like the wandering Jew and turning up in all sorts of places. I have pleasant memories of Byron Bay and remember swimming with a small group of divers who took me out and beneath the rough waters. I did actually hear the whales calling to each other and was enchanted to see a couple of sharks, which it was claimed were harmless, hence the comfortably named 'Carpet Sharks'. After that experience I felt bonded to my little group of divers as if we had shared some initiation but I am only one of the hundreds that are enchanted each year. 'What about shark attacks?' I naturally ask, to which they reply that they haven't had a fatal attack for a few years. Yet I heard about the young man on his honeymoon who was bitten in half while protecting his wife! 'Well, you might get the odd one but it is very rare.' I remember the film of *King Kong* when to appease the great beast a sacrifice had to be offered each year. Perhaps the odd diver has to be sacrificed to the great shark each year as a kind of peace offering. However, I grew to like Byron Bay and its beautiful and abundant nature and its strong hippy will to fend off the developers.

John Bell was waiting patiently in the lobby as I came downstairs to say farewell and we decided, since it was a sunny day, to sit alfresco in the Fountain Café and have a coffee. This is exactly the place we met after I got off the plane, a precise and precious two months ago. Two months ago was the Tyson fight which I saw in the RSL club along with the boozers and poker machines and so Tyson nicely brackets my stay along with the Fountain Café. Two months ago the sun shone as it did today and we exchanged positive thoughts about what we felt we had both accomplished although John far more in that he has to perform it seven times a week. Although that can be Hell at times it is also our drug. John has a slightly Nordic look with his flaxen hair and he is modestly proud of his achievements. It is an unusual pleasure for me to talk to an actor-manager since like the wolf or the tiger we are a vanishing breed. The actor-manager tours with his company and maintains a discipline, which can erode in a show without him present, as a kind of general each night watching his troops. It is something to not only admire but also see the necessity of. We talk of plans and dreams and one of mine was to play Cyrano which he has already done and enjoyed and while I think my shelf date for this role has passed, John, actor-manager, won't hear of it and says, 'Get a good wig, after all, it is a great costume drama!' We exchanged thoughts and ideas to make sure that we would leave a little temptation to come back to and that though time may pass and thousands of miles separate us, there will be a future and we all hopefully will be there to share it. Perhaps an exotic *Midsummer Night's Dream*. John has to be away and auditioning actors for his next sail down the river bard. He looks like a sea captain, staring into the misty distances of his bardic ambitions. I see him dissolve into the distance and become once more part of the throng.

I returned again to the packing and my needless collection of old typed messages the hotel so thoughtfully sends up to your room, so that you might keep a message for years that says 'Susan Chennery is in Richard O'Brian's room, please join us for a drink.' Richard has been holed up in his room for months like a troglodyte, coming out only to be whisked to the set and recording himself on film and then being returned to his room where he strums away at his guitar. Occasionally I would see his tight-skinned, shaven egg of a skull wrapped in even more forbidding black than me, and he seems to have been arrested at a certain age and remained that age for the last twenty years that I have known him. Perhaps he has indeed made some Luciferian pact. I see him at the reception and he is wearing what might be the modern version of a medieval knight's regalia: leather jacket embraced and mottled with silver studs and high boots, which appear to have been deliberately left undone at the top so that they flare out over his equestrian delicate legs. I tell him that I am leaving and he looks slightly bemused since he is dying to leave but cannot until his pact has been fulfilled and he has given his flesh and blood to the film. While I speak, his hawk's eyes pick up the fact that the receptionist has not fulfilled my request which was to leave two separate parcels for two separate people but had put an elastic round both and before I can raise myself like a slug out of the mud of my despondency, he has already instructed her what to do.

I remind myself to give him a copy of *Gross Intrusion* before I leave and take the lift once more to the third floor and get back to the struggle about which bits to throw and which to keep to remind me when back in the cold and damp land. An old message will bring the sunshine back again. And now the phone calls to say that my potential producer is waiting in the lobby and so I am bounced from one to another and each is like a dish that will sustain me in my life's quests. We now venture somewhat closer, to the Vinyl Café almost next door and I am meeting with Mark so as to begin plans to make a life raft that will sail me back to Oz. We decide that it should be *Kvetch*, one of my better oeuvres and a blueprint for anxiety detailing the dreaded disease in all its fascinating manifestations.

As we finish our snack, Rhys Muldoon turns up having just strolled past my hotel and wondered if I might wish to see a movie this afternoon. I feel dumbstruck since something so simple and sweet sounding now takes on the aura of magic, since there is nothing in the world I would rather do than go to a movie and hang out with Rhys and have a good natter but my time is no longer mine but somehow mortgaged to the Fates and they are now leading me to my fate as inexorably as Oedipus being led to his. I tell him the news, that I am going, like one announcing that he has just been arrested (since there your fate is equally in the hands and whims of others) and you are bodily removed from friends, warmth, solace, movies, a stroll to Bronte from Bondi, breakfast at Jackies where the blood has only recently been bleached out of the pavement by the rainfalls of last week. The blood of the poor young Englishman who was carrying his girlfriend's flowers and was set on by a yob whose soul was dead. Poor Brian was slain on that very spot and I can never eat in Jackies without thinking of Brian Hagland. Rhys, who made something of a legend out of his performance in *Decadence*, seems somewhat surprised but to allay his concern I tell him I'll be back very soon, so soon in fact that I leave him my blades to use till I return, since he is always renting his. Please skate in Centennial Park at 6.15 p.m. when I shall be in an air-conditioned tube and I shall perhaps sense it through my feet. I like this park so much, where I have skated many times and know every crack and wobble and only fell once and that was on to the grassy verge.

I crushed the case's lips together and zipped them up and collected all my messages or at least most over the last two months like the Dead Sea Scrolls. It's all done and an hour to go. Susan Chennery arrives to say farewell and she has been an able friend and alert weathervane of the Sydney climate. She's wearing mauve and lilac – a most striking combination. We repair once more to the Vinyl Café and order two more flat-whites and she talks again of her recent dramatic flight to Africa and how much she would like to return there. Also she tells me proudly how well her book is going on the lives of the famous and we salute the minute fulsomely and part. The last person I say goodbye to. It is 4 p.m. and my bags, stuffed full of Australia, are waiting.

I pay my bill and am glad to get out of this hotel at least since I feel I have overstayed my welcome. The sun shines and I am happy since I couldn't have had such an intense day without leaving or valuing people so much. I am going now and walking across the foyer but one more person, a chap called Rob who seems to use the hotel bar a bit like his local and has befriended me, says, 'Hey! Where are you going?' 'I'm off home,' I said but he thinks I said I'm off to Melbourne, to which he replied, 'Have a good time in Melbourne and I'll see you when you come back.' The driver takes me to the airport and I am feeling better about leaving now since it is at least a decision and I do have a home in London. The driver tells me that he left South Africa many years ago – he hated it there and decided to risk it in Oz. 'This place has everything,' he says. Yes, I ponder...

26

'Piss in the Sink Productions'

The Riverside Theatre was a nightmare, mainly to get to through, at 6 p.m., the filthy fog of a traffic choked London, struggling to have what seemed like a gigantic bowel evacuation. In the rush to finish building the theatre on time, little thought was given to the actors (always at the bottom of priorities) as there were no toilets backstage! Hence we rechristened our theatre group 'Piss in the Sink Productions' or 'PITS'. The sink was the salvation for the men, whose built-on attachment allows manoeuvrability. The actresses, bereft of such appendages, had to make sure they went beforehand or would have to suffer the indignity of going in make-up and costume to the public loo.

My two plays, *Brighton Beach Scumbags* and *Sturm Und Drang*, were enjoying a good run on the Riverside's main stage. Four weeks flew past, or rather crawled past, as I oozed through Cromwell Road each night in a slow moving lava trail, a thick, poisonous effluvium and every night I faced the same horrific nose-to-tail. So I'd listen to the theme music from *Last Exit to Brooklyn*, a brilliant, coruscating movie based on Hubert Selby Junior's painful yet moving short stories on New York's low life. Mark Knopfler created the most evocative music that wedded to the film with perfect and utter harmony and brought me back into it each time I punched the cassette into the audio system. The car became a floating bubble of music and I recalled the film's extraordinary savagery interspersed with delicately conceived moments of tenderness. Then, tiring of that, I'd clunk in Phillip Glass's 'Einstein on the Beach' until I could sing along with it. There is a sequence in the piece about a train: an instrument creates the poignant haunting and familiar bellows of a train entering a large city station. A sound that feels almost human, as if the train was uttering its own wounded lament. Then the conductor calls out the names of American cities and each name provokes an emotional response from you. '*New York, Chicago*' he intones with that familiar weariness of one who says this every day, but for us these names summon up magic and extraordinary metropolises that are closer to worlds of fantasy.

So I howl alongside the emotionally wounded train and try to get the same pitch which also acts as a vocal warm-up in my hour-long trek across London. I work through, as I sit there, all the current pains of my life. Ah, at last I can simulate the sound of the train's hoot by really pushing the air through my nose. All around me others are enwrapped in their fish-tanks on wheels but if one of them should idly stray their head in my direction, my wheezing along to 'Einstein on the Beach' may, in fact, appear from their point of view as if I am having a minor fit. However, this puts me in the mood as I slide along Cromwell Road and in this state I have the leisure to study occupants of other cars as they pull alongside. They too are listening to music or radio chat, some nodding to the music's beat. From the outside they also look slightly deranged, nodding aimlessly with a vacant stare into the endless and seemingly infinite view of the backs of cars. Sometimes, like myself, they will slowly turn their heads as they pass a car, a kind of stagnant curiosity, like having the opportunity to stare into a neighbour's window to study them, imagining what they do or where they are going.

A young woman now slowly passes and she is chatting merrily on her mobile. She is using the time well. I suddenly want what I have resisted for a long time – a mobile phone. She looks like an advert for it as she chirps happily away in a traffic jam. She can warn them of her late arrival, anticipate and plan, she seems so self-contained. I continue listening to the sound of the train and howl along with it, getting exactly the right pitch but I have listened too long. With Phillip Glass, the music repeats itself in strange patterns, and you feel almost compelled to play it over and over again, zombie-like, registering its subtle changes that gradually hypnotise you as vast empires and cities roll before your eyes. Whatever is in your mind dances along to the music and so now I am thinking of my future production of *Coriolanus* and I see the great Roman army led by Co-ri-o-lan-us as his soldiers chant his name in the manner of a Carl Orff opera. The music pours into my ears thickened by the imagery that it has glued itself to. Now we creep down Gloucester Road, crossroads of my life, for around this area sits the small, dainty Webber Douglas Academy of Dramatic Art, where I not only studied but learned how to be a director by teaching there ten years later during a fallow acting period. I learned more by teaching and it was there that I began my first experiments with Kafka's *The Trial* in 1967, showing it eventually at the Roundhouse in '73 and finally at the National Theatre in '91. Then I pass the London Academy of Music and Dramatic Art (LAMDA) whose theatre I rented in 1969 and (with borrowed money) staged my first ever production of *Metamorphosis* and fell for one of the secretaries who later ran away with my Polish lodger. So I sit in my tin car offering a passing homage to Annie of LAMDA.

We're crawling along in three lanes at the moment and it might be that one lane surges momentarily ahead offering you a whole new department of faces to study while the rear mirror shows a small snapshot of the one behind. Meanwhile at the same time he studies you in your small front mirror and so everybody is scrutinising each other through these miniature TV-like screens. I pass a pretty woman on my left and ease my foot on the brake a little to be neck and neck and watch her as she elegantly chews a quarter of a prawn sandwich. She pulls away and I see the lady on the mobile phone again still chatting away and it feels as if my life is being constantly recycled before me. I'm on alert as the performance starts at 7.30 and since my watch now says 6.50 p.m. I am ready to cheat, change lanes rapidly whenever I see an opening, be a Jackie Stewart, sneak up on the outside or use a bus lane or ignore a newly born red light but I will not panic until my watch says 7.10 p.m. I won't siphon my nervous energy until that moment. Twenty minutes until panic time. Not long. Good, I'm now in the main stretch before I hit the A4 that leads to Heathrow but I turn off into Hammersmith.

We slow down so much I am able to buy an *Evening Standard* from a street vendor and actually read it between short spurts and it relieves the tension somewhat and makes compelling reading since I focus on the gossipy parts. Sometimes I am left standing and am roused to attention by the car horn behind me. Much of the *Standard*'s gossip is devoted to Princess Di and the book of revelations but I cannot help but think she colluded on it since the day after the book's lurid 'exposures' she was seen coming out of her gym in an incredibly photo-opportunist gym outfit: bare legs, short cycle or work-out pants and cute trainers like she had just worked out and hadn't even bothered to shower unless you come in one gym kit and change into another! She had to know they would be there in their droves and did her boyfriend sell his story or was she in on the act? Like, put that in your pipe and smoke it, Charlie!

The evening is growing darker and the sky is turning a harsh autumn rust. I am getting a wee bit desperate and cut into another lane where I see some space ahead. A woman behind me gives me the finger, which seems unnecessary since she was dawdling and I didn't slow her down but I won't let it annoy me and I swap her finger for a big cynical smile which I hope she can see on my 'TV' mirror. I shot up Pall Mall earlier with no trouble like a fast racetrack. I passed some of my early history at the Institute of Contemporary Arts. It was here I tried out my collage version of *Miss Julie* in the hot, late, summer of 1972. The stage was scattered with leaves and we danced those parts accompanied by cellist Colin Woods whose wondrously sonorous music inspired our moves and gave a haunting accompaniment to Strindberg's high voltage, sexual fable. How wonderful those sweaty nights were and I even did Edward Albee's *Zoo Story* as a warm-up. (Oh, I always overworked and tonight I am, for the first time in twenty years, doing a double bill again by acting in *Sturm und Drang* and *Brighton Beach Scumbags*.) A few years later I performed *The Fall of the House of Usher* there and that time our musician was David Ellis on the harp. So, as I pass the ICA a vibration comes winging back.

To circle Hyde Park Corner is a nightmare. It's like a crazy free-for-all so familiarity has me prepare my car for the centre lane which always seems to enter the maelstrom faster. I wait for the car in front to take the plunge rather like parachuting out of a plane. I wait, shouting unheard instructions to the one in front as the swirling cappuccino of tin and carbon slows down. 'Do it! Go for it!' and then it does and I follow almost challenging those on the roundabout to ram me or let me in. Now we are circling Hyde Park Corner and then I weave my way through the back streets of Knightsbridge threading my car through Ovington Square SW3 where after leaving drama school in 1959 I took a room from another actor who, through circumstances of having high-placed relatives who leased the elegant house, was able to rent out a flat in the basement. I pause sometimes for a few seconds' tender memory since much blood, sweat and tears were shed and much growing-up took place in that basement room; the sweet taste of independence and all the sensations that life brings to a young man in his early twenties. I get an emotional jolt there but drive on through the small charming square and enter Brompton Road. I pass Luba's Bistro where I used to take Annie and where I once threw a cup of luke-warm coffee over a group of screaming Sloanes who had spoiled my meal and was rewarded by a return cup of extra hot coffee on my way out. Luba's was wonderful when Madame Luba presided over the place but now its atmosphere is very different.

Aah, we are getting closer and are in the final lap. The 'Ark', that remarkable building, looms up and I am grateful to make that sidestep into Hammersmith roundabout which presents another thick, nasty stew, another circle of Dante's Inferno but I head left into a remote and run-down part near the river lined with neglected council estates and dilapidated factories and evil little pubs with plastic chairs outside. I speed down and turn into Crisp Road, on to which some joker has added a 'Y'.

Turning into our street where the studio is, I see our actress Kate Carmichael trudging her weary way down this godforsaken and grey London suburb. I park next to Charlie Chaplin's daughter, Victoria, since she and her charming and creative husband, Jean-Baptiste, get in early to prepare for the Cirque Imaginaire. I enter the corridor and then have to fiddle with the code to unlock the backstage door. I then gratefully escape to my dressing room of 'Piss in the Sink Productions' and duly attempt to live up to the title since it has been a long drive. Ah, the luxury of the theatre!

27

Letter from Israel

A nation's taxi drivers may sometimes be a fairly accurate reflection of the mood of the people or even the political health of the state. In Shakespeare's time it might have been its actors since Hamlet implores Polonius to treat the travelling players decently by warning the old man that they are the 'brief chronicles of the time' and it were better to have a bad epitaph when you were dead 'than their ill report while you live'.

London taxi drivers are usually cheerful, phlegmatic, helpful, occasionally prejudiced and sometimes (but rarely) moody and confrontational. They are also quite knowledgeable and philosophic. And one would not quarrel with this as a definition of the British temperament and its government. In Israel, Netanyahu's government is in constant conflict with the Palestinians, with its own people, with the Americans, with the peace accord. Their voices are most often high with rising anger. They seem constantly to be in a race against the ultimate laying down of what borders will be the future state of Israel for all time. Lunatic settlers are dashing to remote hillsides to erect temporary shanty shacks to establish 'facts' before the final Day of Judgement.

In contrast to the British way of life, Israeli politics seems to be playing at fast-forward. The taxi drivers aptly reflect this mood as they drive at insane speeds: abrasive, impatient and always, at least on the surface, seemingly angry. Angry with the world, angry with the traffic, angry that you are not wishing to go where it is convenient but want the suburbs where I am rehearsing *Hamlet*. For them the world out there is the enemy and all the other drivers are 'Palestinians' to be hounded, hooted and raged at and you, the passenger, are a necessary nuisance that they will put up with for a while. Even a car's microsecond pause at the light will provoke him to smash his palm on the hooter whose refrain, like a wolf pack, is taken up by the other drivers. As you walk the streets your mind is pierced at great frequency by the agonised cries of vehicles, stuck or moving as over heated lava, choking, sucking in their own filthy pollution. The general mood is – Don't give in. But the drivers are also fair and demand no tip and once you can penetrate the atmosphere of violence inside the cab they actually are glad to speak.

The noise is all-pervading. Unlike your silent-as-a-hearse, black, beautiful, British cab this is just a car and you are obliged to share its venomous cell of hell with the driver and hear the two-way radio system turned on full blast spewing its shrieking voices at the cabby who is shouting back. Perversely, yet even another radio may be on in the background or he may be shouting into his mobile while the instructions are crackling away like a tank in desert drill. You beg him to lower it a little which he will do without a murmur. They seldom give way to another driver and, if there is a space, are likely to career around at sickening speeds while gravity is pulling your stomach into your spine. They mustn't lose a moment.

The government doesn't want to shed those precious acres not even for peace. Why should we, they think. The land was won as a result of Arab aggression and nobody, except the deceived or prejudiced, can deny that. An aggressor must pay the price. But now it is Palestinians who are paying the price as they see their towns that have been Arab for centuries intruded upon by settlers who seem mostly to hail from Brooklyn or Cape Town and are Jews with the stars (of David) in their eyes. They believe in the Lord of real estate since they quote 'Him' when they claim the land belongs to them. Most of those whom I would consider to be real Israelis – that is, born here and whose parents were born here – couldn't care less and feel that the better the deal for the Palestinians, the better life will be. In their own words: 'Enough, already'.

The new Palestinian airport in Gaza is a source of great pride and when you have a state of your own it becomes precious as you build roads, schools, homes, hospitals and all the makings of sanctuary. When you abide in a stateless murk of shanty life, the only inspiration you have is to one day be a hero to your people and avenge them. By contrast, the settlers are sincere, religious and misguided. They seem to be imbued with a Messianic spirit filtered through post-Holocaust righteousness. Drugged with fervour they left their dreary predictable lives in Brooklyn – travelling the subway and living the ordinary life – to one where an Uzi machine-gun is worn round their shoulders like it might be a prayer shawl. There is a feeling of the Wild West, the holding out against the redskin.

My opinion is that at the moment those who have the most zeal for our Lord are cracking the very foundations of the Israeli state. With a Palestinian state there is a chance for an ultimate, historic destiny between the Jew and Arab. Many Jews dreamed of the greater Israeli state after the Six Day War but then again many more, in the grim ghettos of Europe and before that in the even grimmer shtetls of Russia, dreamed of any Israel at all. Israel is a great and passionate nation but now it must survive the elements within even more than the elements without. By being generous you win; witness the peace with Egypt after trading the Sinai for an historic pact.

I leave the rehearsal room where I am directing *Hamlet* in

Hebrew to open in Haifa in January and the air is balmy and warm. I love to take a taxi to Dizengorf Street and walk back to my hotel passing the cafés and bars and small jewellery shops where, often as not, an elderly Jew is sitting in a small room at the back expertly twiddling with the inside of a watch. Jewellery and tailoring were some of the few trades 'allowed' to be practised by Jews in earlier times in repressive Eastern European countries and so they naturally became adept at them. Through the twinkling lights reflected off the gold I am able to glimpse the past but one hopes there is also a future.

28

The Last Days of a Train Robber

Visited former-train robber Ronnie Biggs in his house in the picturesque Via Allegri, a part of Rio that climbs above the city and twists and turns into a confusing labyrinth of streets. It's my first time back in twelve years and it's the same old place since after middle age nothing changes. The well-used mini-billiard table, though, is now covered up. Biggs's son, the young Mike Biggs, greeted us warmly as did a giant dog the size of a small bus. Mike was a child rock star as a thirteen-year-old, selling millions of records, but as a grown-up his novelty value has sadly worn off but he bravely went out on the road as a 'roadie' to keep his hand in, so to speak. The older Biggs doesn't like idlers.

We enter the domain which is strangely quiet now that the owner has lost the use of speech after a cruel second stroke several weeks ago. He's out of hospital and is nursed at home but still can't swallow food or drink. Some black staff mooch about in the kitchen area and pungent smells of cooking are beginning to fill the rooms.

We sit facing the open window. The sun is already high and throws Mike into silhouette as he entertains us with his adventures and talks with bright enthusiasm about Brazil and the land he wants to buy in the countryside where he can bring up his soon-to-be-born child. He's very grown up now and regales us with stories of the big bash Ronnie had for his seventieth birthday when mates, admirers and others came from all over the world for the three-day ding-dong. Biggs's appetite, like most villains or ex-villains, is immense, I have noticed from my limited association. They seem always to be rebelling against convention even in eating, booze or drugs, as if they were making up for lost time spent eating porridge or in anticipation of the porridge to come. So nothing is restricted and food and booze consumed in vast quantities – enough for an army. Plus no doubt endless supplies of joints; all taken either separately or together.

I first met this outsize personality when sent to Brazil as an actor in a movie so loosely based on his life and alleged kidnap by a mercenary that the real Biggs seemed to fall through the holes. Even so, the film was graced with some talented actors like Peter Firth and Paul Freeman.

The high point was staying at the luxurious Copacabana Palace Hotel along the sea front. This great and majestic white monument to capitalism was created in 1923 and has been home to every species of humanity coming to Rio for whatever desire they happen to cherish and has seen off kings to rock stars. Orson Welles actually lived here for over six months when creating some space between himself and *Citizen Kane*. He was apparently making something a little less controversial – a docu-drama on Brazil and the carnival – but of course it turned sour at the end when the hero of the film, a simple fisherman, was killed by the film crew's boat. The movie was shelved along with 300 cans of exposed film! In the hotel's biography, Rod Stewart is given pride of place for being one of the first guests to actually trash a hotel room by playing football in the elegant aesthetic surroundings and was promptly banned from ever returning. How unsympathetic of them. So once more I can look out upon the giant pool and cast my eyes further on to the

The Last Days of a Train Robber

beach and the limpid blue sea. Having just completed a tour of *Shakespeare's Villains* around South America, I now have a few days off to visit outdoor cafés and drink Brazilian firewater – caipirinha – which over here replaces my old fave, margarita. So pleasant to be able to drink in the warm air and not be ripped off for the pleasure of it.

As I descended the steps to Ronnie's apartment, I recall him saying how he bounds up the steps to get the chore over as soon as possible since he hated them so much. The celebrated train robber, the only one to be caught and then escape, has now been in exile for over thirty years and there is no longer any chance whatsoever of bringing him back to pay his dues. He is a fixture of Rio and a tourist attraction second only to the Corcovada, or giant statue of Jesus, which looms over the city. Tourists regularly ask to meet him and for a price he will give a chat, and sign autographs and T-shirts. I recall him as an ebullient spirit, full of humour and ever ready with working-class abrasiveness and wit. He is the last of the old folk heroes, the outlaws and Western gunslingers. A train robber. A crime of unbelievable daring and audacity. One of the guards was coshed when resisting and it was this blow that was said led later to the man's death which somehow tainted the crime. Of course it was readily seized on but to my knowledge never proved.

Death itself gave Biggs a bit of a tap on the shoulder about eighteen months ago when he suffered a stroke from which he completely recovered and was determined in spite of it not to alter his life style one whit. I mean he has beaten the rap before and why not again. Next time, the long arm of the Grim Reaper was not to be snubbed and struck him down again and a little harder this time. So, unable to speak, eat or drink he is fed through tubes. Nevertheless, a few weeks later he is walking and there is even hope of him recovering some of his faculties.

The old man is now ready to receive us while Mike emphasises that we are the first to be so privileged, and feel somewhat honoured in a funny way. Ronnie enters the room, swathed in a white thick cotton dressing-gown which looks vaguely half-inched from the hospital since it's a couple of sizes too small for his large frame. The tube which extends from his nose has been disconnected and temporarily taped back to his nose so that it can't swing about. A nurse helps him into the room and I get up to take his hand which he grips in a vice of extraordinary power. Is this a signal to me that he is all there and in that powerful grip saying that although there are a few wires disconnected temporarily the battery, which is Biggs, is fully charged?

He sits on the sofa while I try to be as jovial as I know how, reminding him of little events from the past when we filmed here, trying to score the odd bull's-eye in his memory. He dribbles a little since he can no longer use his tongue but is aware of it and frequently, and self-consciously, wipes his mouth. Biggs is a shadow of his former self. I try to raise the wreck of the film *Prisoner of Rio* that was dedicated to him but which was sunk, accurately — torpedoed, by critical response. I start to warm to my theme when we talk of the director. He smiles slightly, obviously liking a human object on which to vent. At a certain story he gives me the thumbs-up. Then, when I was comparing the director's obsession with dozens of takes to wanking (a word I had to learn in Portuguese so I could whisper it under my breath on the set), Ronnie clapped his hands in glee.

Suddenly he cries... almost childlike as if the man had departed, leaving the child unattended. It is a brief squall and lasts only a few moments. It's intensely touching. He can't speak and here is a man who lives though his wit. Mike swiftly comes over and says warmly and firmly, 'Come on Dad, don't cry.' A nurse wipes up the debris the sudden disturbance has caused. He is fine again and grabs a pad and writes down some questions and answers. We manage to communicate now and talk of a mutual party we had in Rio to celebrate my fiftieth and his fifty-seventh. At the time he said, 'Okay, Steve, I'll tell you what, I supply a little band and we'll split the costs,' which seemed reasonable until I realised that I knew only about four people in Rio and he knew hundreds! He smiles at the memory of the easy conquest. Now he is writing at full speed, scribbling page after page and seeming to get actually stronger in front of me. I felt sure that he would recover his speech. What a loss. A painful blow for a born gabber and a man who, as Hamlet says of Yorick, 'could set the table on a roar'.

In some ways Biggs reminds me of those pirates of yore, who gave up their countries, families and safe lives in familiar surroundings to abscond to foreign places, with burning suns, foreign tongues and strange customs. And while not knowing a single word of the language, they knew the ways of humankind in the alleys and back streets of the world. Taking on dark-skinned women, creating a hybrid family and making a new life. A kind of descendant from the *Bounty*.

Biggs is now tired, slowly rises and once more extends the hand to demonstrate his iron grip. It is even stronger as if he wishes to break my fingers. I squeal in exaggerated pain. His nurse aids his walk to the bedroom, and as we part he howls again like a child. I pass his bedroom where he continues to watch the awful Brazilian TV. A group of Afro-Brazilians are still eating in the large kitchen which he made himself since he is an expert carpenter. Our lunch has also been prepared and it's deliciously cooked chicken and roast potatoes and veg accompanied by a salad. The dressing is a give-away: Heinz mayonnaise – an old piece of working-class Britain.

We leave and climb the stairs slowly, not speedily in the Biggs manner, accompanied by a friendly black cat which walks us to the corner as if it was standing in for its master. Yet one cannot help but feel that this is a hint to show us that Biggs still has one more life left.

29
The Killing Fields: Vilnius

Decided to visit the Panerai memorial to the Jews slaughtered there in 1941. Sometimes I think of atrocities as something to do with historical events. It shakes me to think that men, women and children could be murdered while I, a four-year-old, was riding my tricycle around the lounge in an English town.

I was putting off the visit to give myself a whole day there until I discovered it was only ten kilometres outside the city, set in the beautiful Panerai forest. I went downstairs and asked the cabman how much it would be. I had been reading up on Jewish history and learned how the locals in Paunus, hearing the Nazis were on the way and possibly encouraged by some advance PR, took the opportunity to demonstrate their zeal and went out one night and dragged the Jews from their homes and, in one of the most savage orgies of killing since the Middle Ages, put to waste 1500 men, women and children! Apparently they were beaten, raped and killed with whatever the drunken murderers could lay their hands on – hammers, shovels, clubs – and they even amused themselves by pushing water hoses in their mouths and blowing them up. Hell of a night on the town, that was! How much festering hatred over the years could inspire such an act?

After reading that I looked a bit warily at my Lithuanian hosts. I studied their features for signs of barbarism and to my mind these weren't hard to find since this tale had inevitably coloured my view. There was a kind of heavy-jowled, powerful peasant stock, thick-necked, with almost colourless, straight hair and wide, coarse features and yet this same race produced some of the most beautiful young women I have ever seen, strolling proudly in micro-skirts along the streets of Vilnius. Perhaps years of grim Soviet domination relieved only by vodka has had a deadening effect on the populace. Most really were decent people since savagery is always carried out by the minority.

I agreed the price with the cabman of 50 Lits, about £9 return. Unfortunately the driver resembled the type I had in mind since he was large with coarse-looking features, possessing heavy arms and thick fingers and would have been perfect casting for my scenario. We drove silently through the suburbs until the houses thinned out to occasional wooden dacha-like cottages which had an immense summery charm about them. They were not into pretty gardens and flower beds but used them for more practical purposes like raising chickens or junkyards. I had suspected, in some faintly unsettled mood, that the driver knew the area well where I was going. Other tourists would have asked to go there since it was such a famous killing field and I wondered uneasily about his attitude towards it. I felt distinctly uncomfortable with his driving me to such a mournful site.

We turned off the main highway and the thin-treed forest gradually surrounded us and the signs pointed to the word 'Panerai'. He then drove slowly down a narrow road until we stopped at a small square of paving stones. There was a large stone memorial written in Russian and Hebrew but frustratingly not in English. The driver just sat in the car having little English to volunteer any information – not that he seemed to be inclined to. He was just going to wait while I pottered about, took pictures of the memorial and tried to figure out the events that took place on this square. It was not too hard seeing that the railway track runs a few yards away and a few hundred yards from the station. The train would have overshot the local station and stopped here. The trucks would have been opened and the occupants shot fairly rapidly as they ran hysterically in all directions. Few escaped. The memorial must be on this spot for a reason and from what I had read this was my interpretation: some of the guards opening the doors whispered loudly, 'Run quickly for they will kill you.'

I had thought that this small square was it somehow. The driver was just waiting in the car while I self-consciously soaked up the atmosphere, said a little prayer or studied the text. I then decided, in that bright blue and sunny afternoon, to pay him off, and have him out of my cloud and he seemed perfectly willing to accept the half-fare. He took his time before the car slowly drove away. He seemed to have been studying the words on the memorial which I later learned stated that the Hitlerites and their 'accomplices' were responsible. He might have wondered about the word '*accomplices*'.

Now a path led away from the square which I followed although there were no further signs and discovered several more memorials deeper in the forest. So perhaps there were other methods of shooting and killing and the square was a kind of purgatory, a depositing of luggage and carefully packed personal possessions that you were allowed to take, to keep up the con so to speak. 'Just take one suitcase only' and so on.

I had to work this out according to what I had read or knew and could only surmise. I was totally alone here and the day was quiet except for a few birds twittering high in the trees. I try to identify with the events as an actor might. *Am I being shot now? Am I gathered in the square? Or am I simply undressing since the ground was level and the shooters would be in danger of killing each other if they surrounded the victims, that is.* Another path led to a pit surrounded by a huge mound which over the years had grown a fresh carpet of grass and trees and now it became clearer. I learned that these pits were dug by the Russians to be used for storage tanks but they never got round to it. Did the Nazis herd their victims into the pit and then shoot them so the executioners could fire *downward* and not be in risk of killing each other with 'friendly fire'?

Yes, they were led into the pit, killed and then covered with earth and lime and then the next group would be led in; is that it? But then the ground might be loose and uneven and the victims would panic and run, try to clamber out. No, they were cleanly shot in this second square where another memorial stands, impressive and imposing and carved with those majestic and slightly mysterious Hebrew letters. Barricades would prevent them from escaping and a line of soldiers would fire. They fall and are dragged into the pit by Lithuanian workers who place them in layers... Is that it?

The truth is that they were led in groups to the pit's edge and shot and then they fell into the pit, some still breathing, some slowly dying. Perhaps the killers had a system. This might occasionally go awry as when the victims panicked on leaving the train, scattering in all directions.

I stroll into the pit. There is an inscription here which I cannot decipher and this pit has been left just as it was. Later when the Allies were approaching the Nazis made a frenzied attempt to dig up all the rotting bodies and put them in the square in layers with wood between each layer like a gigantic sandwich and then after torching the whole thing pulverised the bones to unidentifiable bits. Perhaps this was one of the incendiary pits since there seemed to be masses of blackened earth mixed with ash as if this had happened yesterday. I learned later that this was where the prison workers were confined but they eventually escaped though a tunnel and now the prison had been destroyed. But there was still something puzzling about the blackened earth. Perhaps after it was destroyed they threw the ashened remains here since it had to go somewhere. Like many before me I thrust my fingers into the earth, just in case my brethren were there and felt I was shaking hands with the past. The earth crumbled and was dark but I continued my search until I felt something between my fingers and it was a tooth! And it seemed to be a back tooth. I pocketed it, believing that it had given me a link to the past.

I examined the other pit and this time walked on the mound surrounding it. I knew what was going to take place and so there was a kind of deliberate calm – well, after all these months it would be over soon. Bullets hopefully will make it quick. I will just accept it. It is a dream. I will awake. If I carry a child he or she too will think it all a dream and that Heaven is coming quickly. I fall into the pit... I see the German soldiers on the hill shooting down, loading and reloading, finishing off the wounded although most of the victims would have been finished off with a bullet to the back of the head.

The blood flows and the bodies pile up. As I look up I can see the sun slowly setting, perhaps exactly as it did 58 years ago. Is that all? Is that possible?

I can still be affected by events that happened 2000 years ago in Masada and here the butchers of Paunus might still be alive!

There are two other pits that have been grassed over in the centre and surrounded by a kind of circular stone seat as if in an amphitheatre where we can sit and watch the horribly obscene drama that unfolds in front of our mind. I stepped over the stone plinth and stood on the grass which was curiously spongy. It would be nice to lay on. Soft and comforting. Strawberry plants are growing just outside the circle. A small spider darts through the grass and as I am not fond of spiders I avoid them and absurdly see it as a Nazi. I don't wish to hurt it and so I stamp my foot. It freezes and shrinks up tightly in a ball of fear and self-protection. Even the spider wishes to live its full life.

The afternoon is calm and the sky a flawless blue. I utter a small prayer and slowly walk away. I walk past the original small square where I now wish the taxi was sitting waiting for me. But a long walk would be good; to meditate upon this terrible event. But it's more than terrible, since an earthquake or the sinking of a ship is terrible. This is beyond words since it is beyond anything that one can imagine, the deliberate, wilful destruction of a part of the human race by other humans. The tearing-down of centuries of culture, learning, wisdom and life. Of destroying the past and leaving nothing. To shoot small children, let alone adults, to commit bestialities that have no parallel.

I walk along the narrow path and I see a couple having a little picnic. Do they come here for picnics then because it is such a charming clearing in the woods? The railway line is on my left and I expect to see a little railway station come into view at any moment and soon I come to the smallish village which is more like a suburb built up with a few Russian-style council flats and some outlying houses. Near one of those wooden storage sheds (which you see near every railway track) are a few depressed-looking souls getting pissed. Obviously this is a meeting place for alcoholics. They all clutch bottles. Further along I see a solitary male standing in front of a wall with a bottle between his lips and drinking for dear life like he was getting a full swig in before having to share it. This is a dead land.

Where is the damned station. It doesn't seem to exist. There is one there but all the doors are locked as if it was dead! It doesn't *want* to exist. Where am I? Why did I dismiss the taxi! I'm lost. Just miles of tracks and industrial wasteland and a closed station. I go to a house where an old man is patching up his garden. 'Excuse me, *Vilnius*?' He turns away and shakes his head. Nobody understands even the word 'Vilnius' for God's sake? There is a little rudimentary snack bar where the woman gives the same bleak response as if there were no such place as Vilnius. Eventually a boy says, 'I speak English.' *Oh thank God*, I think. 'Please, where is the station?' 'Over there, you must cross the tracks.' I look in the direction he indicates and sure enough people are languidly, actually crossing the railway lines. I head back to the tracks and pass the drinkers who are now looking at me with a certain hostility.

    I see a bridge which must take me to another platform since all the other tracks seem filled with giant containers. I climb the stairs and am relieved to see a young woman coming in the other direction so it means there is life and trains do stop here. I walk down the steps from the centre of the bridge since I now see a line that is empty where trains can go opposite ways, but which way? I walk on to the low platform and again plead with the one or two faces that are idly waiting. They wait as if they don't really believe a train will ever come, they wait like life has passed them by. *Vilnius*? They shrug, a limp gesture to the platform. I point. 'Vilnius?' Then I point to the other side and again make the same sound. No, he appears to gesture feebly to the first side. Good. I think so anyway. I am tempted to ask another.

    I hear a train coming and it eventually stops but it is going the other way. It has Paunus boldly on the front. That's where the first killings took place before the Nazis even arrived. *No, I don't wish to go there!* Three or four get on, a few get off. Ignoring the bridge that was built for them they cross the tracks. They cross with a kind of indifference since nobody would really wish to live there who could be conscious of what went on half a mile away. So it's become a poor, downtrodden district where the winos drink near the track. It is the road to Hell and is accursed.

    How long will I have to wait? I feel as if I am in a Kafka nightmare. Everyone is alone on the platform which is only a few inches high. There is no eagerness to be going anywhere, no jabbering on mobiles, or feverish reading of newspapers. They just stand and stare into space. In the far distance I detect a spume of smoke and yes, it's coming in and from our lowly platform the train looks tall, imposing and powerful and it will take me away from this place, please God. I have to climb the steps. I'm on.

The train pulls away but I've no ticket since the station is forever closed. However a ticket collector comes on and sells me a single to Vilnius. I reach in my pocket and offer a 5 Lit note, which is less than a pound. But no, he shakes his head and takes out of my proffered hand 1.60 Lits, which is about 30p. I arrive with some relief in Vilnius. Now I know where Panerai is and will always be – for now unto eternity.

A dying man, a victim of the first pogrom in Paunus, wrote in his own blood as he lay dying. 'Jews revenge! Did he get his revenge? Were they ever punished? Are there some benign old granddads still in Paunus sitting by the fireplace who could tell a story or two...?

30
Stanley Kubrick

I felt very familiar with him and he seemed to encourage that in me. He was genial, fatherly and gentle in his direction. I first did the usual audition since he didn't like to meet the actors except via video and later I learned that I got a part in *A Clockwork Orange*. As parts go, it might be considered a reasonable cameo. Of course I knew of his reputation and adored his films and realised he was one of the greats but felt strangely at peace in his company and at the same time wanted to do my best. We set up the shot. I played a cop, can you believe, for only Kubrick would see me as a young British cop. 'Have a look,' he said and I peeped through the lens. He was keen to show me how the shot would look in very wide angle and I was proud to be shown this respect from such a famous man.

I made sure I knew my lines backwards and inside out. I remember repeating them all day even when not shooting so that they would be always at the front of my mind. On 'Action' I concentrated like never before and on each take was word perfect and 'in' the character. He seemed pleased for he didn't like actors who failed with their lines since he felt they should have done their homework. One actor who kept fluffing his words told Stanley that he didn't like to learn them before coming on the set, learning them through repetition, rehearsal, plotting the moves and so on. but Stanley said that was entirely wrong and that you should know your material so that you can then adapt it to any situation. I made a mental note – not that I needed it since I agreed with Stan. I had two or three days with him and even offered to spit at Malcolm McDowell since the actor playing the spitter seemed low on reserves and so the saliva that runs down McDowells's face in the police station is mine even if you don't see me gobbing. Malcolm warned: 'No stringy bits, please.' Of course I wouldn't. I saw the film a year later and thought it slightly old-fashioned in a charming way. But admired much of it, particularly the use of music. However, I admired the book more.

Several years later I had a call for *Barry Lyndon* and also did my usual video for Stanley and was offered a great role which was then offered to Hardy Kruger but I was content with the smaller role of Lord Ludd. A couple of scenes and some fencing with Ryan O'Neal. By this time I was able to suggest other actors since I knew that he wanted unusual and stage-toughened actors who didn't flinch under pressure. I had been working with my own group of actors and recommended some of them. He took a German actor called Wolf Khaler who gave the kind of very intense performance that I knew he would and Stanley was pleased and grew to trust me more.

I remember flying to Dublin and being called to the set for the preliminary meeting and wardrobe. It was one of those intense stormy Irish nights when the devils are dancing and the wind was howling and the rain pelting down like bullets. Outside a great house in Dublin huge arc lights were being held by strong Irish labourers. They reminded me of the famous photo of soldiers holding up the flag in WWII. It was all so epic outside and expected but as I went inside, the contrast could not be greater. While those poor labourers were freezing and fighting the elements to do their bit for the film,

Stanley was inside having a calm chat with Hardy Kruger who seemed to be having some kind of problem. Actors did feel nervous with Stanley since they were so in awe of him and had such respect (especially after his last great movie *2001*) that they built up a little terror in their hearts and grew fearful before the takes. It was as if they knew that they were party to something that was destined for greatness and buckled a little under the strain. They needn't have worried since most of the characters in Kubrick's movies are subsidiary and curiously two-dimensional types as in *A Clockwork Orange*, apart from the three droogs and even less so in *2001* (apart from the beautiful performance by Keir Dullea) although there were some fine cameos in *Barry Lyndon*.

Basically it was Ryan O'Neal's film plus a stunning performance from Leon Vitali who went on to be Stanley's hard-working assistant after that promising debut. I was now feeling like a Kubrick player and even got bolshy with the make-up and insisted on shaping my own lips as if their crude fingers could not possibly be as skilled as mine – I, the theatre practitioner. I was a bit arrogant in those days but motivated by a fierce pride in serving my master. My costume was sumptuous and I took my fencing lessons seriously for my upcoming duel with the star – even taking subsidiary lessons from an Irish master as well as the studio coach.

My first scene was in the gambling room where the famous Irish actor Patrick Magee (also a Kubrick regular), playing the card sharp, does his fleecing of the aristocrats and was about to fleece me. I am introduced to Patrick who was so brilliant and frightening in *Clockwork Orange* as Frank Alexander. He has to deal the cards and with his dextrous fingerwork deceive us. Also he has a little French to say which is the familiar sound we have all heard: 'Faites vos jeux, mesdames, messieurs.' This is easier said than done since Stanley has an obsession to play with his toys, examining them from all angles and the actor is part of that obsession and after twenty or thirty takes can start losing the meaning of the words he has known all his life. Patrick's eye-patch was wobbling with the increasing nervous strain which looked a little odd in close-up and so Stanley cautioned him gently to keep that eye closed. After a few more takes the French (which wasn't that elegant in the beginning) sounded distinctly weird and was coming out (as Stanley kindly reminded him) as 'Make your eyes' for Patrick was now saying 'Faites vos *yeux*' instead of '*jeux*'. A few more takes... Occasionally Pat would strike a good 'jeux' instead of 'yeux' but then the eye patch would wobble under the immense effort. On a good strike he would get the 'jeux', the patch would be still but the cards would now stick to his sweaty hands, or reluctantly leave them when he is supposed to flick them with the dexterity of a snake flicking its tongue.

A few more takes and acknowledging the problem of achieving all three things – the *jeux*, a still eyeball and a swift expert throw – was a triple not to be seen in this lifetime. Stanley opted for two out of three. He did merely a close-up, leaving the cards delivery for a separate cutaway shot. Consternation. Patrick is not flicking the cards with the kind of expertise Stanley wishes and so he decides to fly in David Berglass, a magician, who has white silken magician's hands. Ah, all is solved. Berglass arrives the next day and is perfectly charming and does all the takes that Stanley needs. But we now see that Pat's great strong Irish paws are hairy and for the next pick-up-shots Pat must (and for the first time in his life!) have his hands shaved! For an actor this might be of little importance but to do it to fit in with your *body double* is a humiliation that I don't think Patrick was able to endure.

Now all attention turned to me. I had been watching the previous day's torture and understood that Stanley needed to see what, if anything, was underneath the actor's façade and was prepared for meltdown if necessary but with the same gently encouraging words. 'It's only a movie, Pat,' he said as we watched Magee's nerves turn to sludge. I was lucky to have just come off the stage and felt a little more confidence and the more I saw my esteemed thespian colleagues succumb, the more the gladiator spirit went into me. I too had some French words plus a certain amount of 'business' playing with the ladies, fawning, kissing hands and general camping about as the effete aristocrat Lord Ludd.

The camera turned its glassy eye to me and Stanley's beady eye was at the end of it. First we did the master – the entire scene with all the business. No problem. I did it, spoke passably good French, played with the ladies, kissed their fingers lasciviously, made my bet after some petulant deliberation and waited for the cards. 'Good Steve. Let's go again'... and again... and again and again. And so it went on and on: changing lenses, positions, panning, moving in, close-up, extreme close-up and each time word perfect. *Not a flutter will he get out of me*, I thought. *No, I will not crumble*. And yet again and again and yet again... and the same or with slight variations. I have set my mind on the scene and am playing a kind of chess game and will not budge. I give myself instructions that the camera will break before I do and even welcome the numbers increasing on the slate. It's a scene with action and tension and he wants as much as he can get. At last he says it's over. I joke to the operator: 'Is that all? I was just getting into it.' With great relief I washed, and with that sense of euphoria that you get on film when you know a difficult part of your life is over, I went to dinner in the hotel and enjoyed my food as never before. Magee passed my table in a sour mood and for some unknown reason threw a few curses my way. Maybe he imagined I was smug. I wasn't, I just seemed to sense the game and how to play it.

The next few days I wandered round the set amazed at the sheer enormity, complexity and profundity of it all. Awed by the technological expertise and somewhat enthralled. The special fast lens needed to capture candle light was imported from America where there was only one other in existence which was used for the Apollo space flight. It had an incredibly short depth of field and so actors had only inches in which they could move forward and back. Hundreds of candles were burning and for continuity had continually to be replaced but Stanley wasn't rushing. Every now and then he took out a little book to check the mathematics of depth of field and light. It seemed all so out of another world. I went to the première and thought it was a beautiful film and, yet again, ever so slightly old fashioned. Seeing it again, as you have to with Kubrick's films, it seemed to grow in stature and caused me to feel that you cannot judge his films in the first showing.

A few years later Stanley called me about *The Shining* but there was nothing in it for me. But having heard about my 'theatre group', he wondered if they would be at all inclined to create a party scene in the hotel fantasy scene where guests come to life. He was reluctant to use extras and wanted actors who although glorified extras would give some life and expertise. Excitedly I put it to the company, also adding that he wanted some topless females. The cast were intrigued by the idea of being creative even in a limited way for him and agreed. I went back and told him that it was on. An assistant then quoted the money. It was marginally more than extras were being paid. In fact he offered us £150 for the week. Each! I was gobsmacked by the smallness of the offer knowing that my team of actors were highly talented and well trained and would do anything and could do anything. He wouldn't budge. Most of them sadly passed on it.

Something strange happens

A couple of years later I received a call from Stanley that left me excited, bemused and utterly mystified. I am, as always, well chuffed to hear from him and curious. He asked me if I knew *The Threepenny Opera*. My heart rose since I not only knew it but had earmarked the role of Macheath for some years now. 'Yes,' I replied cautiously, 'I do know it,' and my mind fast-forwarded and seized on the idea that this is going to be his next possible project and that he wanted me in it! But not to jump the gun I waited. 'Well, I'm thinking about putting it on.' Unusual words for Stanley to use... What did he mean? He continued, 'Do you know that there's a small theatre at the back of Pinewood studios which could be perfect for a try-out?' I was getting confused but trying to analyse the information at speed. Was he going to put on a fringe production of *The Threepenny Opera*? Again he added, hearing perhaps my thoughts between the lines, 'I'd like you to come down if, of course, you're interested, Steve, and audition one of the songs.' Something strange is going on here and I'm trying to figure it out and then Eureka! It slowly hit me – of course! Stanley is such a perfectionist that he wants to try the thing out first to see how it sounds, to get to know the material, to familiarise himself with the texture, to allow the actors and singers to be immersed in it. Aah, I thought, how wise to do this first. And what a brilliant idea since there has been only Peter Brook's less than successful film version in the Fifties.[1] Brilliant, I thought. 'Of course Stanley, I would love to come down and I think it's a marvellous piece.' I ruminated on it and was in no doubt that my interpretation was the right one and that a famous musical needs knowledge and understanding through familiarity. Yes – that must be it. 'I will get back to you,' he said, 'in due course.'

Some weeks later. It was a Sunday as I remember and I was just sitting down to my supper when the phone rang. I was wondering who would ring me late on a Sunday so answered it and an Australian came on the line with quite a pronounced Ozzy accent and you may wonder why this should be of any consequence. She said that she was Stanley's assistant who would be directing *The Threepeneny Opera* and would I come

---
[1] *The Beggars Opera* by John Gay

down to Pinewood for an audition? All matter of fact and assumed. I was astonished, leading to shock, since Stanley had not for a second implied that an assistant was directing this. I was also a mite peeved, leading to some definite anger at the woman on the phone. 'Oh, are you directing it?' I said. 'Oh yes,' she replied. 'Didn't Stanley tell you?' 'And who else have you got on it?' I requested, holding the lid on. 'Well,' she added, 'Stanley's daughter is playing one of the main characters.' Suddenly the penny dropped... or I thought it did. Was this Stanley's way of providing a showcase for his no doubt talented opera singer daughter? How thoughtful and caring of him but no, this was not for me, not with this assistant anyway.

There is a confusion of perception here and no doubt Stanley saw me leading this small band of theatre vagabonds roaming the country that he might call on for a small turn. I said in no uncertain terms that I was not interested in going down to Pinewood to audition for her! End of story. Some days later I received one of his rare letters to me in which he expressed disappointment in me for hadn't I said I was interested etc. and demonstrated enthusiasm and how could I tell his assistant that I now wasn't interested? Also adding that I was a 'weird dude' which I found tolerably amusing. I felt a bit like the old actress in *Sunset Boulevard* who was rung by Cecil B. de Mille because the studio wanted to rent her old classic car and her fantasy led her to unreal pastures. Perhaps I was being used to aid a beloved family member and I too had built up fantasies of playing Macheath on screen directed by Stanley Kubrick. We didn't speak for several years.

Time passed and he seemed to have forgiven me for there was a call, then a murmur of a film set in Poland which could only be about the Holocaust. This of course was shelved. Years passed and again, even after all these years, I am called for an audition via the video for *Eyes Wide Shut*. A small but key role for which he wants me. Now Leon Vitali looking much older and tireder is doing the video. 'He definitely wants you,' I am told. The dates change every week but I am still wanted. I never heard from him again.

31
Reid's Hotel – Madeira

It is hot and I'm in my usual place which is down the long winding steps that lead to the sunbathing terrace overlooking Funchal harbour. The great Victorian Reid's Hotel is perched over a cliff and stands back to allow one of the most exotic gardens on the island to soothe and shade their guests, and of course, if you are on the ground floor, you may open your French windows in the morning to Paradise. The sun is reflected by a billion tiny waves and the sky is washed clean, and perfect blue. I have just swum in the little rock pool that catches the sea's overflow and is a little pocket of the ocean. I'm away from the cinders and smoke of London and the critics who are bent on destroying my play. The sun and sea air puts a veil over the unsightly event. Jack Tinker, of course, rallied round but I fear moribund theatre has coarsened the minds of some of these shallow floggers of opinions. I've been a bit mentally constipated since Wednesday. I deigned to check my script and in my role as the court painter Titorelli, a twelve-minute surreal harangue, I had been saying 'really innocent' instead of 'completely innocent'. This threw me into a quandary of whether I change it back, and now I have to wait a week to put it in. Having decided on a break made me more distressed since I badly wanted carefree days and not to worry whether I change 'really' to 'completely'. Acting is always a chore in the sense that you are always cleaning up your text and pruning embellishments that creep in as if you wanted to get it perfect but it never is. It seems I always need a little something to think about each night before I go on stage to give it an 'edge', some little problem that keeps you 'wound up'. I wonder about all the suffering I give myself in work! You have it 95 per cent right but you will always punish yourself to go for more, like the high-jumper who couldn't reach six foot six but could reach six foot five. For years he was in stress but when he said, 'My goal is six foot four,' he was always happy. Don't make impossible goals.

So even my mini-break has to be perfect. Like the first night in Tenerife when floods of sheer happiness flowed through my whole being, having found the small village, the hotel, the little square and the sangrias...

Hold it, somebody is dying by the pool... I had walked up from the rock pool and decided to take buffet lunch by the big pool and as we sit and eat our delicacies, an old one looks like she's had a heart attack. No one is giving her the kiss of life since they probably don't know or don't care. The sun shines down so brightly now and is so hot that people are somewhat dazed and can't really see that one of the ancient ones has given up.

The old codgers sit around with their elongated British faces and wait for the moment. Few demands for sanitary towels here, I should think. It is a grey society. I believe the woman is not dead but merely in a bad way, probably from sunstroke. The staff are still surrounding her. This is a very Nöel Coward world of silver-encased, thick, white napkins.

We flew Portuguese Airlines and pursued our dream of last year when we went to Reid's for the first time. We selected which swimsuits to take and a young producer came over to talk about a film version of *Decadence*.

The woman is now dying and someone is trying to pump her heart. The kiss of life that someone was brave enough to give didn't seem to work. They are all standing over her... one is feeling her pulse. We continue to eat and politely pretend not to notice that someone is dying by the pool in broad daylight. They try again but have left her too long. The young man is courageous, since muck comes out of her mouth. They take her away but they didn't try long enough. They gave her a few seconds at a time to try inflate her lungs but her heart said a definite 'no'. She died at Reid's. The hearts of the guests continue beating and I continue writing...

Now this block was whether I said 'completely or 'really'. I like a rrrrroll on 'really' and the thing affects me like an unwanted mantra. However, the grass is always greener... so kick it out of the 'Heaven and Hell' syndrome, the wounded warrior syndrome, be a coward sometimes and don't keep challenging yourself, yes, be brave enough to be a coward! The first night at the National I sat in the director's box. I had my make-up on and watched the first act. It looked startling. The safety iron with *The Trial* projected on to it was stunning as it slowly parted like a giant eye opening. It sent shivers up the back of your head. It was so powerful at times that a silence reigned such as I have seldom experienced in the theatre. An awesome silence of sheer fear and wonder, such as you never get in the dead theatre. There you get snores. The first performance I was really angst-ridden and confessed as much to Tony Sher. He said the scene was good. I raced through it scarcely having enough breath to colour the lines but was consumed by a raging fire. The hair of my wig got in my mouth and stuck to my face like the rain on car windows. Nevertheless the first preview went well and we celebrated in the bar. Monday I was uncertain about the wig and took it off and blackened my hair but everybody missed it and I looked too devilish in that Luciferian clichéd expression replete with point at my widow's peak. I kept the wig and glued down the loose strands so I should still look nervy, frazzled, 'artistic', bizarre, and was still breathless but... good... I found it! Was more confident but still my pulse raced before take-off. It was a good night, very good. I started to relax. Frank Nealon suggested changing the lighting in my scene and it felt better and tighter.

Tony gives me an etching or cartoon on the first night. It's me instructing all the actors how to do everything while he stands behind wondering what to do. It's brilliantly inventive, and I'm very proud of such a piece. It's beautifully satiric. T. should take a leaf out of his own book and attenuate his character. Perhaps he will, but too much realism would be the only charge levelled against him. The reviews of course were unbelievably savage. However, I'm glad to be acting again and should keep at it while in the vein. Resist going to New York to direct *Othello* with Chris Walken as Iago. I've had enough of that city for now. Go straight into *Kvetch*.

The clouds on our left hanging over the hills behind the town of Funchal seem to stay permanently there as if to be a constant faucet of rain on the island, soaking up the moisture and letting it out again as if the hills were breathing. Down here by the sea, the sky is empty and clear... just distant puffy clouds hanging on the horizon. Dare I steal some cheese? No, the waiters know.

Decided to allow myself to be a coward and leave the text as it was and not fret at each turn when I know it doesn't really matter. What is shameful is waiting all day to do the scene and then feeling dissatisfaction after. How cruel. What is it? A whisper better... a fraction... the thing is done... forget it. It's over. Rejoice in what you did. When you get back you have plenty of time to worry. I seem to think that by making a decision *for*, my holiday will be better.

Saturday, 9 March

It's a perfectly still warm morning and the sun's standing on tiptoe peeping over the horizon. The gardens sit beautifully laid out as they were a hundred years ago. While the butchery of the 1914–18 war was decimating men, the gardens were being watered and the bushes pruned; while the death camps were in full throttle the clouds gently slid over the sunlit Reid's Hotel and people took tea on the terrace: madness is for other places. It was recently the centenary at Reid's and as the prostitutes were being disembowelled in 1888 in a hideous, dirty, hot August in Whitechapel around the corner from my granddad who claimed he heard the cries, the masons of Reid's were laying the foundation stones for the most glorious hotel on earth, a hotel of gentle luxury and forever smothered gardens of hibiscus and bougainvillaea, Mexican palms and heavily scented jasmine and honeysuckle.

The hotel is only half full and that half are the ancient ones who are well past the stage of fearing terrorists and are therefore not restrained by the fear the younger ones have of the Gulf War. The young are greedy to hold on to their wealth of years and won't take any risks with their youth, whereas the older ones won't give up a delightful winter break at Reid's just because of some dirty Middle East war. All the older ones have lived through the worst war of all time and some were children during the First World War. When you're this age only the yearly pilgrimage to Reid's has any import since Reid's is a signpost that is already halfway to Heaven. The dinner in the grand dining-room is a facsimile of the great astral one. The menu delicate and free from bones, garlic, sauces or any dangerous condiments, herbs or stimuli that might accelerate a modestly beating pulse. Gourmet nursery food but delicious. There is a very good restaurant next door for the more adventurous which Reid's has recently added for the pre-menopausal. But here the soup is a delicate consommé or thick vegetable purée. A light piece of fish may follow, surrounded by little mound of mashed potatoes in crispy jackets. No weird culinary devices, no shells, nothing to crack, no bones to splinter, no porterhouses or entrecôtes to saw, but food that pulls apart, delicate, soft, nothing to crumble those chalky teeth. We don't want a repetition of the poolside in here!

The old are in more abundance this year than last since apart from the fear of flying, many of the more intrepid are taking advantage of the cut-price tours now being offered by most of the under-used hotels. The stalwarts who defended us in the Second World War and come to Reid's have no wish for bargains but want the familiar palace of the great dining-room. They come with their wives or ageing husbands, one supporting the other since by now one has gone into decline, forcing the other to hang in for a while longer and thus be the support for the crumbling mate. It may be that seeing the twilight of their mate has held back their own degenerative effects in order that one should aid the other. Those without partners have surrogate partners in walking sticks but most are couples or even two couples, since most partners have long exhausted any meaningful communication such as might be had by younger married couples. At this age communication largely subsists on where the pills and medicine box are.

Midday. The Pool

I am sitting by a pure blue pool, baby blue or powder blue, the blue of childhood or Wedgwood. The old lady is a memory. The waiter says she was eighty-eight.

'Many deaths here?' I ask, bearing in mind the collected weight of years gathered here at the moment. 'No! No!' he responds emphatically, 'not for years.' There are some distant islands jutting out on the horizon in blue shadows that contain the mystery of unknown lands, jagged, remote and yet full of life.

The Gulf War seems such a puerile anachronism, all those maniacs outdoing each other to get the biggest guns and all that horrendous pollution when Madeira looks a model of tranquil serenity, its brick-coloured roofs rising and falling beneath my panoramic view from the poolside at Reid's. At the next table an English couple are drinking beer in the midday sun and smoking furiously. She gives a hacking cough from time to time. They both look like they have pub binges at home. His face is already burnt but they sit there getting burnt-er!

Everybody here looks, as they walk round the pool in their swimsuits, as if they still had clothes on. Their shapes are pre-war. No one looks as if they have ever exercised beyond taking the mutts for a brisk walk on a damp English Sunday and as they slope round the pool their rib cages seem to sit on their hips. One imagines them like nuts in a shell in which the nuts resemble the shape of the shell and they resemble the shape of suits and ties, collars and jackets. No suggestion of real animal life; all wonky, round-shouldered from desks, spines warped from chairs. Their bodies seem to hang off them like unwanted and undesirable flesh that seems to be some awkward encumbrance. Most of the literature round here, if it can be called that, testifies to the culture and reading matter of the upper classes: Agatha Christie, Len Deighton, Monica Dickens, and one book entitled *The Queen and Prince Charles*. I could see a Kingsley Amis here or a Waugh: belligerent, pompous, nerves frayed from lunch-time booze. The Brits seem to think it awfully *infra dig* to be pissed and loud-mouthed. I suppose it's part of the tradition and even as I write I see that poor John Osborne had to be helped off the stage at the Dorchester, pissed as a newt, at one of the endless award ceremonies when the media congratulate themselves. They sit for four bleary hours smiling at the sight of hacks receiving awards for the drivel that TV has become and feeling well satisfied at being invited to be in the same class of moribundity. No wonder poor John had to get Brahms just to escape the awfulness of it all.

A tall man with one of those extraordinarily British noses produced by careful cross-breeding with aristos, rather beaky and sinister, comes strutting round the pool with his tits hanging down. The waiter strolls lazily up and down waiting for the lunch crowd to avail themselves at the buffet. I wonder what most of these people do for a living, although many look like magistrates.

That evening we walked down the road to the *Doca Docavados*, a charmingly sweet small tower that is now a fish restaurant. It looks like an old citadel or watch-tower and of course is perfectly round. We opened the shutters and sat down to a perfect meal of espinada fish, salad, sangria and yet my head was tossing on the ocean of many possibilities. The wind kept changing direction and flapping the shutters like slaps on the round cheeks of the citadel. The window squared a view on to paradise. A wide sea whose clouds were being drenched in all the colours of a dying sun. And now the distant rock looks as if it has a long alligator pressed to its bosom. Our plates come swimming with sauces, onion, tomato, garlic, and my fish is drowned in it. Sangria pours down easily. The café is deserted since we like to eat early to catch the sun setting over the hills. We kept looking out at the sky to catch each change of picture and I want to drift into the whole experience and disengage my body and float into the ether. But something keeps a little snag in the back of my mind...

Walking into Funchal
The large port town of Funchal has the richness of a balanced and integrated small metropolis, the small side-streets off the beach are teeming rivers of life, wrestling kids, dogs barking from second-storey windows, old ladies leaning over banisters. I pass the open door of a house and inside is a cauldron brimming with life. There are babies being bounced and women doing laundry, a dog sleeping, a young boy playing in the yard, granny in a chair, a seething frenzy of beating hearts.

Life. We hear the tangy vigour of their voices. At the pool we hear the death rattle of upper/middle-class twats with all the juice drained out of them.

WAITER: WOULD MADAME CARE FOR A DRINK?
FAT MADAME: I'M GOING TO BE A BORE AND ASK FOR A SLIMLINE TONIC. (She then piles her buffet plate to the top).

SECOND DRONE: WHAT DO YOU FEEL LIKE DOING, DARLING?
WHINY U/C TART: I'M GOING TO COLLAPSE... (She lies down by the pool)

All these stringy evasive sentences, self-loving and petty. All enthusiasm couched in a language of trivia and nursery talk. Dotty people. We walked right through the town and saw that the community had built swimming pools on the beach made into a concrete oblong box just below the tide level so that in the morning there would be a full pool which would drain out only gradually. We passed the huge sherry brewers where they sold sherry that was a hundred years old and where you could go inside their high-ceilinged warehouses and sample the thick pungent liquor. We bought some lace and imagined the huge houses full of yesteryear life when the plantation owners and sherry distillers lived there in their opulent Portuguese splendour. The sky remains a perfect cobalt blue and C. believes that Gloria Swanson has been sitting at the next table to us at dinner. I saw a *Financial Times* review of *The Trial* and read the scurrilous content and thought I will never ask critics to review a play of mine again.

Critics
The papers have been coming out with reviews of *The Trial* – mostly negative. What bums some critics are, what swinish,

snivelling, uneducated bums who know so little about what the human heart is capable of, the mysteries of the imagination and the skills needed to release that imagination. Their world is limited to the non-imaginative, to what is perceived as reality. Charles Dickens summed it up in a character called Gradgrind, a miserable tyke who seemed to capture well the British trait, or English trait, of only believing in what is before your nose and is real, and the Gradgrind character instructed his harassed pupils not to use their imagination and to denounce anything that wasn't *real*. His puritanism leads him to pontificate that you should only reproduce what is in front of you, so if flowers don't grow on walls or on carpets it's stupid to put them there. Imagination is a sin leading to folly. Is not TV the same, with its trite desire to make TV films about 'corrupt unions' and 'the life of unemployed workers in Liverpool', 'investigation into the police force'? How utterly dreary they all are. These are the ones that watched poor Mr Osborne as he flopped drunkenly off the podium like a rag doll.

11 March

Recovering from the wounds some of those critics gave me. With their poisonous blood one has to be careful not to get contaminated and infected with the hate and bile they inspire. Sloth, bilge and bile, scrawling their weekly graffiti. The low-level expectations have established guidelines. The living dead. I can no longer write about joy, which is what I wish. These ugly, stooped, scurfy mongrels should be ignored.

Monday, Lunch by the pool

Read the *Mail on Sunday*, an affectionate piece both scathing and funny. A whole page helps our spirits: to be damned for daring is intolerable. Then I saw the review in the *Sunday*

Observer written by Michael Coveney and he called the production brilliant, and so was saved by Coveney and was so grateful to him for he is read by many more serious theatregoers then those who read the *Sunday Times*. I was relieved and enthralled, as if somebody had rescued me from the stocks where I was covered in excrement. He had also taken a side-swipe at the 'O' level critics who suddenly became Kafka experts. That's all I needed, one good ally. Of course Tinker helps and his review was so positive, but I am not sure the *Mail* is a 'money review', as the late Joe Papp would say. The *Observer* is, and it is accompanied by a tremendous photo and caption: 'THE MOST SURREAL MIMETIC DISPLAY TO BE SEEN IN LONDON'. Well, I suppose it is all of those things!

The End
Having cappuccino on the terrace outside the Villa Cliff Café, the sun blasts my back as it descends over the palms but the bay is lit up like a new day. It has dropped over the villa next door which looks deserted and beautifully decayed, a few loose slats in the shutters and it's already a worn-out slut. Reid's is lit up by the late afternoon sun and two gulls feed on a fish that one gull had soared into the air with. Having dived like a living spear into the sea, it impaled the fish and then tore it to pieces. At 6 o'clock the sun is still beating down on the promontory that makes Reid's such a perfect setting. The palms dot the cliff face and the garden at the back of the hotel will have its residents out there scooping up the last morsels of sun like hungry cats before dressing for dinner. It's a gala night tonight in the vast expanse of space with its huge ceiling in that imperial design so beloved of great ships like the Queen's and the *Titanic*. We will dress for dinner and have a pre-prandial drink in the bar overlooking the twinkling lights of Funchal. There seems to be a proliferation of lizards this year. They're everywhere, flicking and darting into crevices as you pass by, or watching you, the swift tiny pulse rapidly fibrillating, and ready

to dart off. The mystery islands have disappeared today – quite, quite dissolved in a mist. The sun still beats down but I shift my chair to savour its final farewell. From the terrace of the café must be one of the most perfect sights on earth, just Reid's and the finger of Funchal Bay resting in the harbour. A fishing boat slowly makes its way out. The gulls wheel and spin over the ravine where the strange crabs live, and large unfamiliar birds sit for hours barely moving and knowing everything they need to know. They are like grey stones resting on the cliff face. They will no doubt be there next year like the guests of Reid's, ever faithful to their Madeiran sanctuary.

32
Rio 2000

First, let's park the car a couple of miles at least from the Copacabana since they expect quite a few people to swell that famous avenue – 3 million to be precise, give or take a hundred thousand or two. We all dress in white since this is the required mode to celebrate the sea goddess Ijemanja as we throw flowers into the grasping waves. With high spirits and expectations we walk swiftly to our destination, an apartment bang in the centre of the Copacabana commanding a magnificent view of the Millennium fireworks display which is rumoured to be colossal. Preparations have been under way for some time and every few hundred yards of the avenue there are stages roped off upon which we see some innocuous looking parcels. They could be broken-down, neglected graveyards. But these sleeping parcels will explode into a pyrotechnic fantasy in a few hours' time – all worked, of course, by remote control. Only a couple of security guards drift lazily around the area.

It's just 6 p.m. and as we stroll along the avenue the sun is still gloriously high in the sky, burning brightly as if saluting the final day with as fine a show of fiery power as it can summon. It's a flawless, slowly setting orange ball surrounded by a few obeisant, fluffy mashed potato clouds, perfectly formed pillows like one used to see more of in one's youth or in children's fairy tales. The day is expectant as Rio is preparing herself for the night but steadily, slowly, streaming out of the suburbs, the city, the favelas, picturesque- (from a distance) looking slums that tumble down the hills surrounding the city. All heading down to the beaches, to Copacabana and Ipanema particularly. Three million they estimate in totality. An improbable amount and barely imaginable.

    We stroll past little huts which are dotted every few yards like filling stations to serve the needs of the beaches. For their size (no more than a small kitchen) they seem to serve an impossibly large amount of produce, from hot dogs, sandwiches, beers, margaritas and juices to cigarettes; while outside and hanging from every hook are scores of coconuts. A giant fridge takes up half the hut where coconuts are served *gelado* (chilled) but demand today is outstripping the speed at which they can chill them. Walking leisurely, the adoring sun caressing our necks and backs, we stop off at one of the little kiosks since this is part of the ritual and order our coconuts. He cuts one off a hanging branch and, holding it steadily in one hand, uses the other to grip a deadly sharp machete. Whack! He brings it down swiftly, aiming the blade into the neck of the coconut, turns it a little and then renews the attack. The top is prised off. I'm relieved that the blade doesn't slip... A straw is stuck in and, *voila*, you have your ready-made fruit juice: sweet, milky, bland, nutty.

    We slurp our coconuts dry and head into the main Copacabana avenue joining an army of white shirts, pants and skirts. The ample arses of the women are squeezed into their skirts revealing every shape of panty line. They are mostly cut very high giving the arse an artificial line as if it tapered down from the top of the hill to the crotch in a neat little triangle ignoring the rest of the blubber that hangs loose, like the line was wishful thinking. Since all are going in one direction we face a sea of arses that swing: arses whose cheeks seem to be in battles with each other, young cheeky arses, virginal arses hard as billiard balls, ancient arses, all moving, all in white, and all heading towards the beach and at the same time each scrutinised by, examined by, ogled by, dismissed by, categorised by, desired by thousands of male eyes.

After a few thousand arses we suffer from eye fatigue and stop this time for a corn on the cob that's piping hot, wrapped in banana leaves soaked in butter and sprinkled with salt... Crunch, the taste invades the mouth like its life blood was soaking into you; you bite down and shred a few golden nuggets off the spool and chew them as the skin rams itself between your teeth. The sun is still beating your back and as it slowly sinks, it harmonises with the taste: irresistible, sensual. Now the sun is crawling into a huge bed of cloud and as it does everybody around us claps in gratitude for giving us yet again another brilliant, hot, luscious, life-giving day. As it disappears it sends its farewell in a deep orange glow for some time yet.

Slowly we are making our way to the destination, drinking in the sights and savouring the last of '99. In doorways the poor are sheltering from the heat, their children's heads lolling in the late afternoon's drowsy sun. What care they for New Year celebrations or Copacabana parties where frenzied black staff are preparing the catering for their spoiled white masters? Young rippled teenagers wearing just singlets and trunks or just tiny swimsuits strut down the streets; some are without shoes but their shiny young muscles dance defiantly. Some have come from the favelas which are being drained of their youth as everybody pours like lava on to the two beaches. A lava of flesh, a lava-flow of pounding, expectant humanity.

The streets are warm and full of smells: rich smells, fruity smells, flower smells, human smells and urine smells. Caretakers lean against the metal gated doors leading to rich air-conditioned apartments, shadowy lobbies lined with leather sofas. They gossip or sit on chairs outside just keeping an eye out for which service each tenant willingly pays but I have heard that sometimes a thief will pay ten times more for him to nod off for ten minutes. Now we're right on Copacabana beach and the crowds are building up and the sea of white has dark patches in it. Concert platforms have been erected every hundred or so yards and the bands are tuning up. Rock and roll, jazz, Brazilian *batteria*. Here you have a line of drummers thwacking in unison as they test the sound system. It sends a huge shock wave through me which temporarily melts my civilised veneer and sends me careering back in time. We pass on. The waves fade in the distance.

Another break. One feels one must taste and try and savour everything tonight. A cheese stand where tasty squares of cheese are heated over small braziers and then, when hot and melting, are pierced by a stick. Too delicious, oh scrumptious, oh delicacy, oh feast!

The crowds are heading towards the wide beaches bringing their wine, beer, picnics, boxes, hampers, armfuls of kids or just themselves. All are drawn magnetically to what will be or promises to be the biggest event in Rio's history and the biggest fireworks display in the world. It promises to dwarf London since it can be contained in a relatively defined area and will be Promethean, volcanic, epic as if some great god will open his jaws on the magic moment of midnight and celebrate the anniversary in a mockery of the Earth's creation.

Most small vendors have left their pitches in the surrounding streets and headed to the beaches which are now littered with thousands of little stalls lit by small kerosene burners. I imagine the dutiful women in the favelas preparing the prawns, the mussels, the chicken wings and sausages which are now sizzling temptingly on the little grills. Giant coolers are offering beer, lagers and colas. The round huts meanwhile are selling everything as if beneath the ground was a giant well of infinite depth. Here you can buy whiskey, vermouth, gins, and the best, the most piquant, the most delicious, burning, insatiable, the raw juice of the cane – Cachasssa! It's mixed with freshly crushed limes, cracked ice and stirred with a scoop of powdered sugar. Oh heady, bittersweet, toxic, powerful fire-water.

The sky now begins its epilogue, its dying crescendo in a blazing inferno of colour while the wall of white now extends as far as the eye can see. We reach the elegant apartment house where scores of people seem to have gathered, some just to see who is coming in since this is where the ritzy folk live. Others are trying to gatecrash one of the many parties that are going on since each floor is celebrating the Millennium with its unsurpassed view. Since the natives of Rio are famous for gatecrashers as well as for producing astute thieves, we clutch a plastic card that identifies us by colour-coding. The crowd surges forward as someone with the correct credentials is allowed into the hallowed temple. The bodyguards cross their arms over their chests, unconsciously symbolising the entrance they are determined to protect. We are waved in by our host Dietrich Batista who is well known to them and the muscled wall parts for a moment. I can feel the crowd anxious to squirm into the temporary gap, pretending to be part of our little group but the breach is swiftly sealed off again. The lift is ever busy and so we walk up the eight flights of stairs and as we ascend we are able to view through each open door the furious preparations for the parties. Busy black or Indian maids are dragging boxes of fruit that are stored on the staircase; mounds of strawberries, heaps of papayas, mountains of tomatoes and meanwhile squeezing past us are streams of young girls, eyes ablaze to find the right party.

At last we arrive and gasp at the epic view from the panoramic windows that stretch across the whole apartment. We make the usual party twitter until the countdown while we watch the swell steadily growing, the white increasing, the dark patches decreasing and reaching as far as the eye can see. Yes, there has to be millions gathered here and never before have I been able to witness approximately one and a half million people in a continuous sea of flesh from one end of the Copacabana to the other. One great river of white and yet unseen but just round the corner in Ipanema is an equal vast river of white totalling up to three million. Titanic, colossal!

We continue our party chatter but everything said seems to diminish against the enormity of entering the year of Two Thousand. We are introduced to strangers who all seem to hail from Germany or at least descend from there while black servants silently pad in and out bearing titbits. We wander round while children bounce between the adjoining rooms. I lean over the balcony and see below the crowd outside the doorway of the apartment growing larger and more intense like supplicants worshipping at the orifice of the rich. Like flies round meat. Yet people are still pouring into all floors, filling up steadily like the *Titanic* filling up with water. A TV soap star must have entered since the crowd gives a whoop of joy as a young man strides in terribly self-importantly followed by his entourage of shrill and shrieking female mouths.

Now the countdown begins and the wall of white stretching out to infinity has now reached right down to the beach and to the waves licking gently in. It could be an ice-capped sea moving almost imperceptibly. Small cracks appear in the white as the crowd shifts slightly but these get sealed up almost immediately. The natives are getting both excited and impatient and so a few freelance firecrackers are thrown, just to ease the tension and singe the air. We wait for those boxes, those magic boxes on the beach to detonate. It is now 11.40 p.m. and the street lights are suddenly turned off... a great roar from the crowd. This is a sign preparing us for the Big One and no drippy street lights are to upstage what is to come. Or even deflect it a whisper.

Such a crowd. It invites comparisons. I could imagine that this huge crowd in white have been gathered together for execution. Double it and it resembles that terrible number that is forever seared in our brains and that we are not allowed to forget. The thoughts as quickly dissolve since we are entering 2000 and the century of bloodbaths must be over and we are entering with clean hands the next one. My watch says two minutes to go and I realise that London has already done it! At 8 p.m.! My heart goes out to it. It's getting loud and suddenly I am aware of a strange sound... it's the crowd beginning a great deep roar: from man to man, to woman to child, it gets louder, it grows, it cannot subside, it's waiting to burst, it's agonising, dying to be born. THE MILLENNIUM CHILD IS GROANING TO EXPLODE OUT OF THE PEOPLE! Even if it really is the last year of the last century it heralds the birth of the twenty-first. It's bulging, it's soaring, howling, heaving, crying: tears prick our eyes and run down our cheeks. The first batteries of fireworks explode into the night...

OH! OH! OH! OOOOH! say the crowd and OH! again and again and again and once again as each blast, each effulgent explosion exceeds the last, firing off with such speed that one salvo is already burying itself into the fading inferno of the last and so the dark night air is always full. Barely before that umbrella of fiery raindrops has plunged into extinction another spears its bright meteor into the soft belly of the night and then as it reaches its apogee it spends itself in a bright, brilliant, orgasmic umbrella. The crowd wails, wows, whooshes, is satisfied, exhilarated... I'm reminded of something else: missiles and anti-missiles, the Gulf War and how pretty war looks on TV, how like a great fireworks display, and how everything reminds us of something else. We are at peace, we are amazed and stand still, worshipping in the new mewling enfant 2000.

And then, and then it stopped! Quiet again, and again a few last sputterings from individuals and then over. The post-coital trudge home. It's starting to drizzle and we walk back through the sludge, the mashed-up containers and cartons and old cardboard that was somebody's home, past the families sheltering in the doorways with their sleepy ones, past the corn on the cob sellers, past the last of the vendors trying to keep their old wares looking fresh, past 1999 but still, nothing, nothing will ever compete with the arrival in Rio of the year 2000!